USING LOTUS 1-2-3

A How-To-Do-It Manual
for Library Applications

ROBERT MACHALOW

*HOW-TO-DO-IT MANUALS
FOR LIBRARIES
Number 1*

Series Editor: Bill Katz

NEAL-SCHUMAN PUBLISHERS, INC.
New York, London 1989

Lotus 1-2-3 is a trademark or registered
trademark of Lotus Development Corp.

Sideways is a trademark of Funk Software, Inc.

Published by Neal-Schuman Publishers, Inc.
23 Leonard Street
New York, NY 10013

Copyright © 1989 by Neal-Schuman Publishers, Inc.

All rights reserved. Reproduction of this book, in whole or in
part, without written permission of the publisher is prohibited.

Printed and bound in the United States of America

Library of Congress Cataloging-in-Publication Data

Machalow, Robert.
    Using Lotus 1-2-3.

    (How to do it manuals for libraries ; no. 1)
    Includes index.
    1. Libraries—Automation. 2. Lotus 1-2-3 (Computer
program) I. Title. II. Series.
Z678.93.L68M33 1989   025′00285   88-31410
ISBN 1-5557-0033-0

TO ROSALIE

CONTENTS

	Series Editor's Preface	7
	Preface	9
Part I	Lotus 1-2-3: The Program	11
	Introduction	13
1	Worksheet	17
2	Range	22
3	Copy	25
4	Move	27
5	Review	29
6	File	34
7	Print	36
8	Graph	39
9	Data	43
10	Formulas and Functions	46
11	Review	49
12	Command Summary	54
13	Macros	57
Part II	Library Applications	63
	Introduction	65
14	Department Budget	67
15	Book Budget	74
16	Library Budget	77
17	Budget Request	79
18	Timesheets	83
19	Circulation	85
20	Overdues	98
21	Periodicals	103
22	Reference	113
23	Database Searching	118

24	Software Evaluation	130
25	Shelving	140
26	Indexes	147
27	Catalog Cards	153
	Index	163

SERIES EDITOR'S PREFACE

You are reading the first manual in a series of how-to-do-it guides for librarians and students. No more fitting work could lead the series. It offers a forthright, easy-to-follow map for those who wish to use the spreadsheet program Lotus 1-2-3 in the day-to-day operation of their library. This guide is a particular joy to this reader because of its clarity and accessibility—rare qualities for an escort through modern technology.

We know all too well that there exists in the world a dazzling amount of information which the lay person can't use because it cannot be understood. All too often, the manuals that are supposed to explain the products of the new technologies seem designed to obfuscate.

I am here to report that Robert Machalow has defied the rules. He has written a book that offers a readable, logical explanation of the topic. Both beginners and near-experts will find much here to put them at ease. His calm, clear approach helps to overcome the computer phobia that bothers so many.

First, Machalow provides the grounding in Lotus necessary to follow the argument, and then he develops the internal architecture needed for library problem-solving. The logic of his approach is one of the most valuable aspects of this guide. Equally important, of course—and unique to this book—is that the examples given are for libraries. It is supposed, of course, that the user has the Lotus files at hand and has some basic appreciation of what they can and can't do in the library.

After spending time with the explanation of the basics in the first section, the reader can then move on to the second part. Here are area-by-area uses of the software in the library. Whether one is laboring at the reference desk or working on a budget, Lotus offers ways to do work faster, more efficiently, and with considerably less effort.

One of the most fascinating discussions concerns how Lotus can be put to work teaching. I'm not sure that this makes shelving any more a delight, but at least it does explain why Melvil Dewey and the Library of Congress spent so much time trying to get it right. The slave Lotus is even called up to show users about the library.

The new technology does benefit people and need not be the high road to a migraine. In explaining Lotus, the author succeeds in showing both its ease of use for novices and its range for the experienced. It is a lifeline to spreadsheets, graphics, and databases.

This guide is a mature, evenly balanced exposition of how one method can save time and make life in the library better for everyone. It is a marvelous beginning for a series that aims to do just that in every area of library activity.

Bill Katz

PREFACE

Most librarians are not computer programmers. So, like most computer users, librarians have to rely on software created by others. Librarians have been bombarded with offers for software packages that do some very specific things: one package can handle the circulation area, another will handle budgets, and still a third can aid library patrons in discovering how to use the library.

Instead of a multitude of software packages, one particular piece of software can be used to do all the above, and a lot more. Lotus 1-2-3 has three integrated functions: spreadsheets, databases, and graphics. By using these three functions, a librarian can create files to aid him or her to more productively use time.

Before actually using Lotus 1-2-3 to accomplish specific tasks, the user should learn some of the commands, formulas, and functions of Lotus. To accomplish this, each chapter in the first portion of this book discusses a command, or the formulas and functions of Lotus. Practical, library related examples are used throughout. In addition, review chapters are provided to give the user hands-on, practical experience with the creation and use of library-related Lotus files.

A chapter on macros is also included. A macro can combine all of the information of commands, formulas, and functions into an automated way to accomplish various tasks.

Part two then takes the information from the first part and applies it to specific library situations. First, four types of budgets are examined: a department budget, a book budget, a library budget, and a budget request.

Then, timesheets are explored. In many libraries, there are several part-time workers, and keeping track of their time can be time-consuming.

Next, Lotus files that keep circulation records and print overdue notices and that compute overdue fines are discussed.

Reference and serials departments are then examined. Reference statistics are tracked and graphed. A method of automating a periodicals holdings list is suggested. An on-line file of a library's journals holdings is also created.

Database searching statistics are evaluated by a Lotus spreadsheet. Then a tool for evaluating the value of library computer software is described.

Lotus is then used as an instructional tool. Educating workers in the order that books should be placed on the shelves is often difficult. Shelving is taught using Lotus macros and the database functions. Finally, Lotus is used to help to educate library users. Indexes are explained through a thorough examination of a specific index entry; catalog cards are explained through an in-depth examination of the contents of a catalog card. Each educational section utilizes numerous macros to accomplish their goals.

Each of the sections in the second part can be used exactly as they are presented; in addition, suggestions for modifications are given so that each can be used in a variety of library settings. Modifications are also suggested so that any release of Lotus can be used for each of the applications.

Many people have helped me in creating this work: Judith Bartlett of York College's Business Office helped me with some of the trickier Lotus commands and functions; David Goetz of York College's Academic Computing Department gave me a great deal of help with equipment and programs; Che-Tsao Huang, Chairman of York College's Academic Computing Department, also aided me with my equipment requirements; and Edward Kalaydjian, York College's Business Manager, deserves a special note of thanks: Ed introduced me to Lotus many years ago. Of course, the person who gave me the most support throughout this endeavor has been Rosalie Machalow, my wife.

Robert Machalow
York College
City University of New York
Jamaica, N.Y.

PART I

LOTUS 1-2-3: THE PROGRAM

INTRODUCTION

Lotus 1-2-3 is a powerful program that has been used for several years in businesses around the world. It is possible to use this program productively for spreadsheets, databases, and graphics. *Using Lotus 1-2-3* will introduce you to the functions of Lotus and detail several specific library applications of the program.

The book is structured in two parts: the first provides an overview of the basic commands, functions, and formulas that can be used with Lotus; the second part details specific library applications, explaining the logic of the formulas as well as how they can be modified to fit your own library's needs.

Before beginning the mastery of the features of the program, it is necessary to learn how to move around a worksheet. In Lotus, there are several ways. To illustrate them, it will be helpful if you work along on Lotus and construct a very simple weekly schedule using Lotus.

First, load Lotus. After following the prompts, you will be confronted with a screen that is blank except for a row of letters spaced near the top of the screen, and a column of numbers along the left side. This is a blank worksheet.

Figure 1

```
FIGURE 1

A1:                                                              MENU
Worksheet  Range  Copy  Move  File  Print  Graph  Data  System  Quit
Global, Insert, Delete, Column, Erase, Titles, Window, Status, Page
         A        B       C       D       E       F       G       H
 1
 2
 3
 4
 5
 6
 7
 8
 9
10
11
12
13
14
15
16
17
18
19
20   Blank worksheet with menu choices    (/)
24-Mar-88   10:08 AM
```

Each location on the worksheet is called a cell, and cells are identified by a combination of the letter (indicating the column) and a number (indicating the row) of the location. Thus, the cell in the upper left hand corner is identified as A1. The simplest way to move from one cell to the next is to use the arrow keys. Each time you depress an arrow key, the location of the highlighter (also called the cellpointer and the cursor) will move one cell in the direction of the arrow key that you depressed. This is a slow but very reliable way to move around a small worksheet.

Using this method, fill in the days of the week along the first row, starting at cell B1. Cell B1 will be labelled MON, for Monday. To fill in the cell, simply type MON; MON will appear above the column headings in an area called the control panel. MON will stay in the control panel until the cursor is moved or the enter key is depressed. Then, to move to cell C1, depress the arrow key pointing to the right. The highlighter (cursor) moves to the right one space, and the typed MON appears on the worksheet in cell B1. Fill this cell with TUES, for Tuesday. Then depress the arrow key pointing to the right and continue by filling in WEDS (D1), THURS (E1), and FRI (F1).

Now move the cursor to the upper left hand corner of the worksheet (cell A1). You can do this by depressing the arrow key pointing to the left several times, or you can use a shortcut: depress the key marked "home." On many keyboards, this key is also the number 7 key and can be used as the home key when the Num Lock is off. At any time during a session, you can return the cursor to the first cell (A1) by depressing the home key.

Another way to move the cursor to this position is to use the function key F5. This key is the "GOTO" key. The program will ask for a location, and in this case you would simply type A1 and depress the enter key; the cursor will move to cell A1. This is a very convenient feature, since it will allow you to move anywhere on a worksheet quickly.

Another way to move the cursor is to use the key marked "end." This feature is a little tricky as it must be used in conjunction with one of the arrow keys. When the end key is depressed followed by an arrow key, the cursor moves to the last filled-in cell in the direction in which the arrow is pointing. If there is a blank cell, the cursor will stop directly before it. This feature is convenient when you are trying to fill in blank spaces in a worksheet. In this case, you could have depressed the end key, and then the arrow key pointing to the left. The cursor would have appeared in cell B1, and then you could move it the final space with the arrow key.

Along the left-hand column (column A), you should fill in times.

Move the cursor from one cell to the next using the arrow key, filling in cell A2 with '8:00 (the ' is a label prefix which is necessary to allow you to use a colon; otherwise, the program will not accept a cell which begins with a number and has a colon in it. This prefix also justifies entries to the left hand margin of the cells).

If you continue entering times on a half hour basis, your worksheet should look like Figure 2.

Figure 2

Now you can practice using the different ways of moving the cursor around the worksheet by filling in the following:

    Monday 9:00: Meeting
    Tuesday 10:00: Ref Desk
    Friday 1:30: Book Talk

Did you use the function key F5 (the GOTO key)? Practice using that key as well as the arrow keys before moving on to the next chapter. Lotus allows very large worksheets: the earlier versions allowed up to 256 columns and 2048 rows; the more recent versions allow up to 256 columns and 8192 rows. Clearly, with the

```
FIGURE 2

A1:                                                              READY


         A        B        C        D        E        F        G        H
1                 MON      TUES     WED      THURS    FRI
2        8:00
3        8:30
4        9:00
5        10:00
6        10:30
7        11:00
8        11:30
9        12:00
10       12:30
11       1:00
12       1:30
13       2:00
14       2:30
15       3:00
16       3:30
17       4:00
18       4:30
19       5:00
20       5:30
24-Mar-88   10:05 AM
```

Figure 3

larger worksheets the short-cut methods of moving around can be of great value.

```
FIGURE 3

A1:                                                              READY


         A         B         C         D         E         F         G         H
 1                 MON       TUES      WED       THURS     FRI
 2       8:00
 3       8:30
 4       9:00      meeting
 5       9:30
 6       10:00               ref desk
 7       10:30
 8       11:00
 9       11:30
10       12:00
11       12:30
12       1:00
13       1:30                                              book talk
14       2:00
15       2:30
16       3:00
17       3:30
18       4:00
19       4:30
20       5:00
24-Mar-88  10:04 AM
```

1 WORKSHEET

Once you have become familiar with what a worksheet is and how to move around it, it is important to understand the command structure of Lotus. At any time, it is possible to enter the command menus by depressing the / key. Also, at any time, by depressing the function key F1 you can receive help.

When the / key is depressed, two lines of text appear on the top of the screen in the control panel: the top line is the menu, and the one underneath either refers to the submenus associated with the highlighted menu item or explains the menu choice.

Figure 1-1

To make a menu selection, you can move the highlighting with the arrow keys, after which you will have to depress the enter key; otherwise, you can simply depress the key that corresponds to the first letter of the selection that you wish to make. In this case, the enter key is not depressed.

In the next several chapters, each of the more important menu selections will be discussed and illustrated when necessary. Each menu selection performs a different function.

Worksheet: The first possible menu selection is WORKSHEET

```
FIGURE 1-1

A20: 'Worksheet menu choice (/w)                                      MENU
Global  Insert  Delete  Column  Erase  Titles  Window  Status  Page
Set worksheet settings
        A       B       C       D       E       F       G       H
1
2
3
4
5
6
7
8
9
10
11
12
13
14
15
16
17
18
19
20   Worksheet menu choice (/w)
02-Dec-88   07:25 PM
```

18 USING LOTUS 1-2-3

(referred to as /w). Most of the changes made to a worksheet by using these commands affect the entire worksheet and thus should be made with care.

When WORKSHEET (/w) is selected, eight submenu choices are presented: global, insert, delete, column-width, erase, titles, window, and status. Several of these are further subdivided.

Figure 1-2

Global (referred to as /wg): The first of the submenu choices is used primarily to make changes that affect the entire worksheet. Each of these will be discussed separately.

Format (referred to as /wgf): This selection formats the entries for all the cells on a worksheet. There are nine possible formats, including fixed, scientific, currency (which would probably be used in a budget worksheet), "," (which simply inserts commas where they would normally be placed if you were writing figures such as 1,000 or 1,000,000), general (the decimal format), +/-, percent, date (there are several date possibilities), and text (which displays formulas rather than cell values). In the later releases of

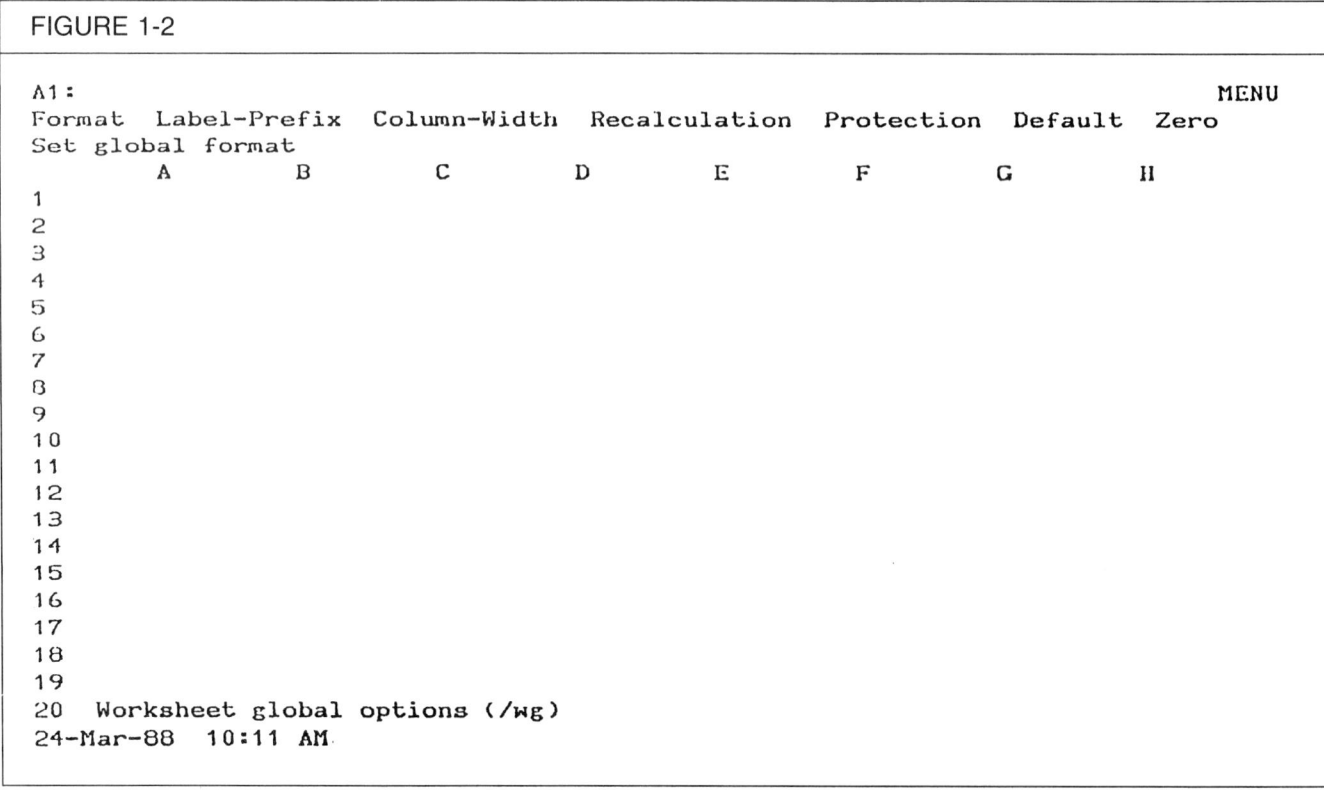

FIGURE 1-2

Lotus, two other formats are offered: hidden (which suppresses cell display) and display (previously hidden cell displays).

Label Prefix (referred to as /wgl): This command aligns the information placed in each cell to the right margin of the cell, the left margin of the cell, or in the center of the cell.

Column-Width (referred to as /wgc): This command changes the width of the columns of the worksheet. If no changes are made, the default width is nine. Often the format selected determines the minimum column width. If the column width selected is not sufficient for the contents of the cell, Lotus will display a cell filled with *****.

Recalculation (referred to as /wgr): There are several subdivisions of this, including: natural, columnwise, rowwise, automatic (which is the default), manual (which should be used for a lengthy worksheet, since each time a cell is added or modified, the entire worksheet is recalculated in the automatic default setting. With recalculation set at manual, you can quickly make all the modifications and/or additions that you need to make on a worksheet and then depress the recalculation key, which is the function key F9), and iteration.

Protection (referred to as /wgp): Protecting a worksheet prohibits changes from being made. This option is useful to protect formulas. Often, you will not want to use this command; instead, you will want to protect a certain range of cells rather than an entire worksheet. This command permits protection to be either enabled or disabled.

Default (referred to as /wgd): The default disk and printer setting can be changed using this command. Using the command /wgdd (worksheet global default disk), you will probably want to change the default disk from A to B if you are using Lotus on a two-disk system: this influences which disk is saved to and retrieved from, and in a two-drive system, your Lotus disk will be in drive A and your data disk in drive B. After changing the default drive, you will then update by using /wgdu (worksheet global default update), which will permanently change the default settings.

Zero: The more recent releases of Lotus have one final Global choice: ZERO (referred to as /wgz). This command turns on and off zero suppression.

In addition to the choice of global, seven other submenu choices are available in /w (worksheet).

Insert (referred to as /wi) is used to insert either columns or rows into a worksheet. It is usually necessary to insert columns and/or rows when moving information around a worksheet. When you insert a row or column, Lotus will automaticallly readdress all formulas in affected cells on the worksheet.

Delete (referred to as /wd) is used to eliminate columns or rows from a worksheet. These can be either blank or filled in columns and/or rows. If worksheet delete (/wd) is used on cells that are not blank, the information will be deleted and lost.

Column-Width (referred to as /wc) permits you to modify the width of individual columns. The default width is nine. Two additional choices are available on the later releases of Lotus: hide (which prevents viewing of specified columns) and display (which permits the viewing of previously hidden columns).

Erase (referred to as /we) erases the entire worksheet. If the worksheet has not been saved prior to this command, it will be completely lost (more about saving files later). This command is useful after you have used a worksheet, saved it, and wish to use another worksheet. It is also useful when you are designing a worksheet: sometimes you may want to start from scratch.

Titles (referred to as /wt) allows you to keep titles on the screen even if the length and/or width of your worksheet extends past the borders of the screen being displayed. To activate titles, place the cursor in the row and/or column under and/or to the right of the portions you wish to keep on the screen continually. Then use /wt; choose horizontal, vertical, or both.

Window (referred to as /ww): Using this command, it is possible to divide the worksheet in two parts, and either view both parts at the same time or jump from one part of the worksheet to the other simply by depressing the window key, the function key F6. The windows can be either horizontal or vertical and can be either synchronized or unsynchronized.

Status (referred to as /ws) shows you the settings that are currently activated as well as the amount of memory currently available.

Page (referred to as /wp) inserts a page-break marker onto the worksheet. This option is only available on recent releases of Lotus.

2 RANGE

The second menu choice is RANGE (referred to as /r); many of the submenus in Range are similar to those in Worksheet. The only difference is that while the commands in Worksheet will usually modify the entire worksheet, the commands in Range will modify only a specified cell or range of cells.

Figure 2-1

Format (referred to as /rf): this command modifies only specifically designated portions of the worksheet. As in /wgf, the formats possible are: fixed, scientific, currency, ",", general, +/-, percent, date, and text. The more recent releases of Lotus have two additional choices: hidden and display.

Figure 2-2

Label Prefix (referred to as /rl): This command allows the user to align the specified text to the right, left, or center of the cell.

Erase (referred to as /re): This will erase a specific cell or range of cells; it is not used to erase an entire worksheet (for erasing an entire worksheet, use /we).

```
FIGURE 2-1

A1:                                                                    MENU
Format  Label  Erase  Name  Justify  Protect  Unprotect  Input  Value  Transpose
Format a cell or range of cells
          A         B         C         D         E         F         G         H
 1
 2
 3
 4
 5
 6
 7
 8
 9
10
11
12
13
14
15
16
17
18
19
20   Range menu (/r)
30-Nov-88   10:19 AM
```

Name (referred to as /rn): This is used in relation to range names. The possible submenu choices are: create, delete, label, and reset. Label names are often created and used so that when writing a statement, formula, or macro you will be able to use the name of an item or range instead of trying to remember the exact cell location. In addition, this command is used to name macros.

Another use for this option is to move around the worksheet quickly. By naming a specific cell with the range name create command (/rnc), you will be able to get to that cell by using the range name and the GOTO key (the function key F5). Using a name that is easy to remember (such as the column heading name) will be simpler than remembering the cell address.

Justify (referred to as /rj): This command adjusts the width of text.

Protect and Unprotect: PROTECT (referred to as /rp) and UNPROTECT (referred to as /ru): These commands are used to protect (or to take away the protection of) individual cells, col-

---

FIGURE 2-2

```
A1:                                                              MENU
Fixed   Scientific   Currency   ,   General   +/-   Percent   Date   Text   Hidden   Reset
Fixed number of decimal places (x.xx)
         A         B         C         D        E         F         G         H
 1
 2
 3
 4
 5
 6
 7
 8
 9
10
11
12
13
14
15
16
17
18
19
20    Format options (either /wgf or /rf)
24-Mar-88   10:15 AM
```

umns, or rows. To protect an entire worksheet, you would use the worksheet global protect command (/wgp). The protection of a cell or range of cells prohibits the user from making any changes to the protected area. The command is usually used to protect formulas and macros.

Input (referred to as /ri): This command can be thought of as being similar to the range protect command (/rp) in that it prohibits the user from altering the indicated range of cells. But the range input command is more than that: this command actually prevents the user from moving the cursor to the protected range of cells. This sort of protection is sometimes desirable.

Value (referred to as /rv): This option is used to copy the contents of a cell, but not the formulas on which the contents are based. This option is only available on the more recent releases of Lotus.

Transpose (referred to as /rt): This option copies ranges, switching columns and rows. This option is not available on the earlier releases of Lotus.

3 COPY

Lotus has a menu option for copying information or formulas contained in an individual cell or range of cells: COPY (referred to as /c). When copying textual information (such as column headings, titles, etc.), Lotus simply duplicates the cells involved. When formulas are copied, several things can happen, depending on the cell address(es) contained in the formula.

Lotus has three types of cell addresses: relative, absolute, and mixed. An example of each will help in describing the differences involved in the three types of addresses as well as the copy command.

Given the formula +A2+B3+B4 in cell C4, the copy command (/c) will transform the formula from cell C4 to cell C5 as +A3+B4+B5. Both parts (column and row) of the addresses indicated in the formula in C4 are relative, and they change as the cell is copied.

If you do not want the cell to be relative, you can fix the location of both parts of the address (the row and column) by placing a $ before each part. Thus, instead of +A2+B3+B4 in cell C4, the absolute addresses of the cells would be +$A$2+$B$3+$B$4. With this formula in cell C4, the copy command would simply copy the cells' addresses as they are, and cell C5 would also contain +$A$2+$B$3+$B$4 after the copy command was employed. Thus the address is absolute.

In a mixed address, one part of the address is absolute and the other part relative. It would not matter if the column were absolute and the row relative or the other way around. Still, the address would be mixed and the /c command would retain the absolute portion while modifying the relative portion.

When the copy command (/c) is used, Lotus will ask for the cell or range of cells to be copied. You can either describe the locations with cell addresses or enter the point mode of Lotus. To use the point mode, place the cursor at one end of the range of cells to be copied, then depress /c. Depress the period (.), which anchors the end of the range, and then use the arrow keys to indicate what cells need to be copied. As you use the arrow keys, the cells that you wish to be copied will be highlighted. When all the cells have been highlighted, depress the enter key. You will then be prompted to describe the cell(s) to be copied to. Once again, you can either describe the cell's or range of cells' locations, or use the point mode to indicate the location to which you wish the copying to be done. Only the upper left hand cell of the range to be copied to needs to be specified.

The point mode can be very helpful, especially since errors can occur in writing the addresses of cells. The GOTO key (the function key F5) can be used to quickly get from one location on the worksheet to another, making the pointing easier on a larger worksheet.

The copy command is also used when you want to underline an item such as column headings. First, you would depress the \ key, which tells Lotus to fill the entire cell by repeating the next key. To underline, you would first depress the \ key and then the - key. Depress the enter key, and the cell will be filled with underlinings. To underline all the items on that particular row, depress /c and then copy the cell that was underlined all the way across the worksheet.

A suggestion: when you know that you will be using the copy command to copy the contents of a cell, and after you have finished typing the contents of the cell, use the enter key rather than an arrow key. This way, when Lotus prompts you for the address of the cell from which you wish to copy, you can once again simply depress the enter key. Similarly, if you plan to copy a range of cells, depress the enter key after the last one has been typed. When Lotus prompts for the address of the cells to be copied, you can enter the point mode (by depressing the "." key) and then simply use the arrow keys to highlight the cells to be copied from. Finally, depress the enter key.

4 MOVE

The next menu possibility is MOVE (referred to as /m). This command does exactly what it says it does: it moves information from one part of the worksheet to another. After depressing /m, you will be asked to describe, in terms of cell address or range of cell addresses, which cells you wish moved. Then you will be asked for a location to which you would like the cells moved. You can enter the point mode to describe either the move from or the move to location. Lotus will do the rest for you.

One note of caution: you must either have or insert a blank row or column where you wish to move the information to; otherwise, you will lose the information originally contained in those cells. To insert either a row or a column, you must use the worksheet insert (/wi) command.

For example, if you had the accompanying worksheet, you could make various changes without having to do the tedious job of reentering data.

Figure 4-1

In the above worksheet, it might be easier to compare the number of reference questions asked at the two desks if the information in columns B and E were placed side by side. To

```
FIGURE 4-1

A1: 'REFERENCE STATISTICS                                              READY


         A         B         C         D         E         F         G         H
 1  REFERENCE STATISTICS
 2            DESK ONE: Books            DESK TWO: Periodicals
 3            Ref       Direct    Other    Ref       Direct    Other
 4   Jan      232       433       231      201       303       334
 5   Feb      323       455       300      301       354       467
 6   Mar      444       432       398      569       309       331
 7   Apr      333       532       367      560       456       379
 8   May      761       699       400      598       678       562
 9   June     667       709       349      801       809       421
10   July     222       144       132      213       107       120
11   Aug      199       122       104      178       103       104
12   Sept     256       333       157      298       401       321
13   Oct      341       345       225      378       320       348
14   Nov      401       444       248      478       504       602
15   Dec      445       401       389      569       601       589
16
17
18
19
20
27-Mar-88   02:28 PM
```

27

accomplish this, you would first insert a blank column between columns B and C, then use the move (/m) command, detailing the range to move from as E3..E15. Then depress the enter key. The move to range would be specified as C3..C15 (the column which you inserted as a blank column). When you depress the enter key, the two columns of information with the reference statistics are together. You can repeat the procedure to move the columns of statistics about directional questions as well as the columns of other questions asked.

The worksheet with all the moves will look like Figure 4-2.

Figure 4-2

Unlike the copy command (/c), the move command does not modify cell addresses. The move command (/m) simply moves the contents of cells, including formulas, as written.

```
FIGURE 4-2

A1: 'REFERENCE STATISTICS                                              READY


           A          B        C        D         E        F        G        H
 1   REFERENCE STATISTICS
 2              Ref        Ref       Direct    Direct    Other    Other
 3     Jan      232        201       433       303       231      334
 4     Feb      323        301       455       354       300      467
 5     Mar      444        569       432       309       398      331
 6     Apr      333        560       532       456       367      379
 7     May      761        598       699       678       400      562
 8     June     667        801       709       809       349      421
 9     July     222        213       144       107       132      120
10     Aug      199        178       122       103       104      104
11     Sept     256        298       333       401       157      321
12     Oct      341        378       345       320       225      348
13     Nov      401        478       444       504       248      602
14     Dec      445        569       401       601       389      589
15
16
17
18
19
20
27-Mar-88   02:33 PM
```

5 REVIEW

To review the options of the first four menu choices, construct a worksheet showing the number of books acquired, the number of catalog cards produced, and the cost by the month for the years 1985, 1986, and 1987. The months should be listed down the left hand column. The three headings should be across the top.

Some suggestions that may help you:

Adjust the widths of each of the columns that will have headings: the default setting of nine is probably not enough if you do not abbreviate or use more than one line for each of the column headings. To do this, you will probably use the /wc (worksheet column-width) option for each of the columns individually. On the other hand, you could use /wgc (worksheet global column-width) to adjust all of the columns at one time, and then adjust the left hand one to be narrower by using the /wc (worksheet column width) on that column alone.

Use /wgl (worksheet global label prefix) or /rl (range label prefix) to align the columns to the right, left, or center of the cells.

You will want to format the column for currency, which will record the cost of the books. This is done with the /rfc (range format currency) command. Since the worksheet will be more than 20 lines in length, you should use /wt (worksheet titles) to keep the titles (column headings) on the screen even though the rest of the screen will scroll up. Place the cursor in cell A2, then use /wth (worksheet titles horizontal). If you do not do this, you may get confused when entering the information.

At this point, you probably have a worksheet that looks very similar to Figure 5-1.

Figure 5-1

Now that you have the worksheet, the following information can be entered (remember to use the arrow keys as well as the GOTO key—the function key F5—to move around the worksheet):

Books acquired, 1985: January, 125; February, 221; March, 345; April, 221; May, 198; June, 145; July, 102; August, 97; September, 143; October, 197; November, 234; December, 243.

Books acquired, 1986: January, 132; February, 156; March, 199; April, 225; May, 231; June, 132; July, 99; August, 78; September, 133; October, 178; November, 200; December, 278.

Books acquired, 1987: January, 101; February, 199; March, 233; April, 246; May, 245; June, 167; July, 100; August, 122; September, 144; October, 176; November, 189; December, 297.

Cards produced, 1985: January, 650; February, 735; March, 1835; April, 1321; May, 987; June, 876; July, 698; August, 578; September, 708; October, 1320; November, 1387; December, 1402.

```
FIGURE 5-1
                Books           Cards           Cost
                Acquired        Produced
      1985
           Jan
           Feb
           Mar
           Apr
           May
           June
           July
           Aug
           Sept
           Oct
           Nov
           Dec
      1986
           Jan
           Feb
           Mar
           Apr
           May
           June
           July
           Aug
           Sept
           Oct
           Nov
           Dec
      1987
           Jan
           Feb
           Mar
           Apr
           May
           June
           July
           Aug
           Sept
           Oct
           Nov
           Dec
```

Cards produced, 1986: January, 657; February, 760; March, 507; April, 1230; May, 1302; June, 698; July, 498; August, 345; September, 674; October, 709; November, 808; December, 1098.

Cards produced, 1987: January, 498; February, 910; March, 1109; April, 1130; May, 1128; June, 1078; July, 908; August, 987; September, 689; October, 780; November, 789; December, 1288.

Cost, 1985: January, $1405; February, $3021; March, $4320; April, $3289; May, $2878; June, $2098; July, $1679; August, $1398; September, $2145; October, $3198; November, $3345; December, $3756.

Cost, 1986: January, $2434; February, $1876; March, $3345; April, $3345; May, $3402; June, $2430; July, $1509; August, $1087; September, $2405; October, $3679; November, $3098; December, $4032.

Cost, 1987: January, $2087; February, $3450; March, $3650; April, $3507; May, $3480; June, $2109; July, $987; August, $998; September, $2650; October, $2340; November, $3210; December, $4998.

After entering all the above information, your worksheet should look similar to Figure 5-2.

Figure 5-2

Several adjustments could be made in the worksheet for the sake of clarity. First of all, having the years 1985, 1986, and 1987 next to each other would be helpful. To do this, use the move command (/m). Indicate the information from 1986 and 1987 separately, since the moves will be accomplished in separate steps. Also, indicate where you want them moved.

Placing the years above the column headings would be advisable. To do this, you would have to clear the titles (/wtc) and then insert a row above them. First, though, you may want to add a title. To do this, you should insert two rows. Use the /wir (worksheet insert row) command.

Now, starting at cell A1 type a title. Technical Services Statistics: 1985-1987 works well. Before typing the years in the second row, delete the lists of months from the information for 1986 and 1987. To do this, use the column delete command: /wdc (worksheet delete column). Indicate the two columns to be deleted. These deletions will have to be accomplished separately. You will notice that the remaining information moves over. (If you did not want the information to move over, you would have used the /re, range erase, command which simply erases the contents of specified cells.)

Now you are ready to complete the column headings for the three years. In the second row, type the years in cells B2, F2, and I2.

32 USING LOTUS 1-2-3

```
FIGURE 5-2
                    Books        Cards           Cost
                  Acquired     Produced
      1985
       Jan          125          650         $1,405.00
       Feb          221          735         $3,021.00
       Mar          345         1035         $4,320.00
       Apr          221         1321         $3,289.00
       May          198          987         $2,878.00
       June         145          876         $2,098.00
       July         102          698         $1,679.00
       Aug           97          578         $1,398.00
       Sept         143          708         $2,145.00
       Oct          197         1320         $3,198.00
       Nov          234         1387         $3,345.00
       Dec          243         1402         $3,756.00
      1986
       Jan          132          657         $2,434.00
       Feb          156          760         $1,876.00
       Mar          199          507         $3,345.00
       Apr          225         1230         $3,345.00
       May          231         1302         $3,402.00
       June         132          698         $2,430.00
       July          99          498         $1,509.00
       Aug           78          345         $1,087.00
       Sept         133          674         $2,405.00
       Oct          178          709         $3,679.00
       Nov          200          808         $3,098.00
       Dec          273         1098         $4,032.00
      1987
       Jan          101          498         $2,087.00
       Feb          199          910         $3,450.00
       Mar          233         1109         $3,650.00
       Apr          246         1130         $3,507.00
       May          245         1128         $3,480.00
       June         167         1078         $2,109.00
       July         100          908           $987.00
       Aug          122          987           $998.00
       Sept         144          689         $2,650.00
       Oct          176          780         $2,340.00
       Nov          189          789         $3,210.00
       Dec          297         1288         $4,998.00
```

Figure 5-3

Then use the copy command (/c) to copy the column headings for the columns for 1986 and 1987 from 1985.

Now use the /wt (worksheet titles) command to keep the months of the year on screen even though the worksheet exceeds the width of the screen. To do this, use the /wt (worksheet titles) command. In this case, you can place the cursor at cell B2 and choose vertical, which will keep the cells to the left continually on screen. An added benefit is that it will also keep the worksheet's title continually on

FIGURE 5-3

TECHNICAL SERVICES STATISTICS: 1985-1987

	1985 Books Acquired	Cards Produced	Cost	1986 Books Acquired	Cards Produced	Cost	1987 Books Acquired	Cards Produced	Cost
Jan	125	650	$1,405.00	132	657	$2,434.00	101	498	$2,087.00
Feb	221	735	$3,021.00	156	760	$1,876.00	199	910	$3,450.00
Mar	345	1035	$4,320.00	199	507	$3,345.00	233	1109	$3,650.00
Apr	221	1321	$3,289.00	225	1230	$3,345.00	246	1130	$3,507.00
May	198	987	$2,878.00	231	1302	$3,402.00	245	1128	$3,480.00
June	145	876	$2,098.00	132	698	$2,430.00	167	1078	$2,109.00
July	102	698	$1,679.00	99	498	$1,509.00	100	908	$987.00
Aug	97	578	$1,398.00	78	345	$1,087.00	122	987	$998.00
Sept	143	708	$2,145.00	133	674	$2,405.00	144	689	$2,650.00
Oct	197	1320	$3,198.00	178	709	$3,679.00	176	780	$2,340.00
Nov	234	1387	$3,345.00	200	808	$3,098.00	189	789	$3,210.00
Dec	243	1402	$3,756.00	273	1098	$4,032.00	297	1288	$4,998.00

Worksheet printed using Sideways

screen since the title was typed in cell A1. In other cases, you would use /wtb (worksheet titles both) to keep both horizontal and vertical titles on screen.

6 FILE

The next menu option, FILE (referred to as /f), is very important: once you have created a worksheet, you must save it before the computer is turned off or it will be lost. In addition, if you want to modify an existing file, you must be able to retrieve it. These functions, among others, are available through the file menu option.

Figure 6-1

Save (referred to as /fs): At any point, you can save a Lotus file with /fs. If the file you are working on is a new file, you will be asked to name it. If the file is one that you are revising, you will be given the option of using the same name (if you choose this option, Lotus will ask if you want to replace the existing file) or giving the file a new name. After the name is entered, depress the enter key, and Lotus will save the file. You will remain on the worksheet so that further modifications can be made if you want. If you then wish to use another worksheet, use the file retrieve option (more about the file retrieve command later).

On the more recent releases of Lotus, it is possible to limit access to a saved file by requiring a password. When you do this, though,

```
FIGURE 6-1

A1:                                                              MENU
Retrieve  Save  Combine  Xtract  Erase  List  Import  Directory
Erase the current worksheet and display the selected worksheet
          A       B        C        D       E      F       G        H
 1
 2
 3
 4
 5
 6
 7
 8
 9
10
11
12
13
14
15
16
17
18
19
20   File menu (/f)
24-Mar-88  10:17 AM
```

you will only be able to retrieve the file with that password. There is no way to recover the password, so if you forget it, the file will be totally inaccessible. To save a file with a password, follow the procedure above (/fs), type the file name, space, and then p. Depress the enter key. Lotus will then prompt you for a password. This password will not appear anywhere, but it is necessary to have it in order to gain access to the file.

Retrieve (referred to as /fr): This option allows you to retrieve an existing file. Simply type /fr and Lotus will give you a list of existing files. You can choose to view one of these by either typing the name of the file you wish to work on or by moving the highlighting to the appropriate file name. In either case, depress the enter key. The file will be displayed on the screen.

It is always wise to save the current worksheet prior to manipulating it with any of the following options.

Combine (referred to as /fc): This command is used to combine a worksheet or part of a worksheet into the currently displayed worksheet.

Xtract (referred to as /fx): This command saves a portion of the current worksheet as a separate file. The saved portion can then be used easily with /fc (file combine).

Erase (referred to as /fe): Files of a particular type (worksheet, print, or graph) can be removed using this command. The file is erased from the disk and cannot be retrieved. Related to this command are /we (worksheet erase), which erases the worksheet from the display but retains it on the disk, and /re (range erase), which erases specified cells from a currently displayed worksheet but retains them on the disk.

List (referred to as /fl): The names of worksheet files, print files, and graph files can be listed separately by using this command.

Import (referred to as /fi): This command is used to incorporate a print file into the worksheet. Files created with some programs can be imported using this command. With earlier versions of Lotus, the translation utility is used in place of /fi.

Directory (referred to as /fd): This option displays or sets the current directory.

7 PRINT

Another of the menu options is PRINT (referred to as /p). In order to get a printed copy of a worksheet or portion of a worksheet, it is necessary to invoke the print command. You can only print the currently displayed worksheet, so if you want to print one that is in memory, you must first use the /fr (file retrieve) command, name the file that you wish to have retrieved, and then use /p (print). Lotus will prompt you to find out whether you want to print to a file (referred to as /pf) or to a printer (referred to as /pp). If you choose printer, you will be given a submenu with several choices, one of which must be completed, others of which are optional.

Figure 7-1

Range (referred to as /ppr): This command defines the area of the worksheet that you wish to have printed. You must specify a range, even if you want the entire worksheet printed. You can describe the worksheet area in terms of cell addresses, or use the point mode. To use the point mode, it is usually wise to place the cursor in the upper left hand corner of the portion of the worksheet that you want printed (if you want the entire worksheet printed, simply depress the home key), depress the "." key to anchor the highlight-

```
FIGURE 7-1

A1:                                                              MENU
Range  Line  Page  Options  Clear  Align  Go  Quit
Specify a range to print
         A        B        C        D        E        F        G        H
 1
 2
 3
 4
 5
 6
 7
 8
 9
10
11
12
13
14
15
16
17
18
19
20    Print printer menu (/pp)
30-Nov-88   10:19 AM
```

36

ing, and then use the arrow keys or the end key and the arrow keys to highlight the portion that you wish to print.

Line (referred to as /ppl): This command advances the printer one line. It is useful to use this command to separate one printout from the next by inserting a blank line (or several blank lines) between them.

Page (referred to as /ppp): This command advances the printer to the top of the next page. It is most often used after printing a worksheet so that the next document printed will be at the top of the next page.

Options (referred to as /ppo): There are several options available: header, footer, margins, borders, setup (font size and style using setup strings), page length, and other (which allows the print to be either as displayed with numeric values or the formulas that make up each of the cells, as well as formatted or unformatted in terms of page breaks, headers, and footers).

```
FIGURE 7-2

A1:                                                              MENU
Header  Footer  Margins  Borders  Setup  Pg-Length  Other  Quit
Specify header line
        A       B        C        D      E          F      G     H
1
2
3
4
5
6
7
8
9
10
11
12
13
14
15
16
17
18
19
20   Print printer options menu (/ppo)
30-Nov-88  10:18 AM
```

Figure 7-2
Figure 7-3

Clear (referred to as /ppc): This command clears all previous print settings.

Align (referred to as /ppa): This command informs Lotus that you have aligned the top of the page on the printer.

Go (referred to as /ppg): After all the other commands have been completed, this command tells Lotus to actually go ahead and print. Remember: prior to go (/ppg), the only mandatory submenu option is /ppr, which specifies the range to be printed. Be sure the printer is on prior to /ppg.

```
FIGURE 7-3

A1:                                                              MENU
As-Displayed  Cell-Formulas   Formatted   Unformatted
Print range as displayed
         A         B         C         D         E         F         G         H
 1
 2
 3
 4
 5
 6
 7
 8
 9
10
11
12
13
14
15
16
17
18
19
20   Print printer options other menu (/ppoo)
30-Nov-88  10:20 AM
```

8 GRAPH

Lotus allows you to represent information on a worksheet as five different types of graph: line, bar, XY, stacked bar, and pie. With some configurations of machinery, you will not be able to view the graph, but by using the PrintGraph disk of Lotus, you will be able to print whether or not you can view.

Figure 8-1

Graph (referred to as /g), another of the menu options, has many submenu choices. The first, type (referred to as /gt), represents the type of graph you wish to construct. This one seems simple, but in many ways it is a crucial decision: some information is better emphasized by a different type of graph than others. Experiment with the different types of graphs and then choose the one which best suits the purpose of a particular presentation.

Type (referred to as /gt): This command allows you to choose the type of graph to be constructed. The possible types are line, bar, XY, stacked bar, and pie.

The next seven submenu choices (X,A,B,C,D,E, and F) are used to represent the ranges for each of the graphs. Generally, graph

```
FIGURE 8-1

A1:                                                            MENU
Type  X  A  B  C  D  E  F  Reset  View  Save  Options  Name  Quit
Set graph type
         A         B         C         D         E         F         G         H
1
2
3
4
5
6
7
8
9
10
11
12
13
14
15
16
17
18
19
20    Graph menu (/g)
30-Nov-88   10:21 AM
```

ranges should be continuous; having blank cells between values usually is not a good idea.

Line graphs (referred to as /gtl) can have between one and six different values represented. To choose the ranges for a line graph, use data ranges A through F if you want to have six ranges represented. If not, choose only the number of ranges that you need.

Bar graphs (referred to as /gtb) can also represent up to six values. If all six values are on one range, use only the A range; if more than one range is used, employ the appropriate number of ranges A through F.

XY graphs (referred to as /gtx) employ the X range for the values to be plotted on the horizontal axis; the A range is used for values to be plotted on the vertical axis.

Stacked bar graphs (referred to as /gts) are a variation of the simple bar graph (/gtb).

Pie charts (referred to as /gtp) use the A range.

Reset (referred to as /gr): This command is used to cancel the range settings described above.

View (referred to as /gv): This command allows the viewing of graphs with certain hardware configurations. If viewing is not available for the configuration that you are using, don't worry: you will still be able to print graphs. Of course, it is easier to adjust the graphs before printing, but some things are not possible with some configurations.

Save (referred to as /gs): The settings chosen will be saved in a graph file with this command. In order to print a graph, it has to be saved first.

Options (referred to as /go): The options included are: legend, format (used only for line and XY graphs), data labels, titles, grid (not available with pie charts), scale, color (only available with color monitors), B&W (used only if you have a color monitor and have previously indicated that you wanted to change from color to black and white).

Figure 8-2

Name (referred to as /gn): This command permits more than one graph to be stored with one worksheet. If you try several different graph types with the information from one worksheet, you should use this command to name the several graphs.

After the graph settings have been saved, you can print the

FIGURE 8-2

```
A1:                                                                    MENU
Legend  Format   Titles   Grid   Scale   Color   B&W   Data-Labels   Quit
Specify data-range legends
           A         B         C         D         E         F         G         H
  1
  2
  3
  4
  5
  6
  7
  8
  9
 10
 11
 12
 13
 14
 15
 16
 17
 18
 19
 20   Graph options (/go)
 30-Nov-88  10:22 AM
```

Figure 8-3

graph. You must exit from the Lotus System disk (/qy: quit yes) after saving the graph settings (/gs). Then choose PrintGraph from the opening screen. On a two-drive system, you will then be prompted to replace the Lotus System disk with the PrintGraph disk. Do so, and depress the enter key.

The opening menu of the PrintGraph disk is comprised of six options: select, settings, go, align, page, and exit.

Select: This option permits you to choose the graph to be printed. Lotus searches the disk for files marked with the .pic extension, which connotes graphs. You can choose any graph to print.

Settings: This option will not be used very often, since it is only necessary to change settings if the configuration of your hardware changes. The first time you use PrintGraph, you should select this option first.

Go: This command actually tells Lotus to go ahead and print the selected graph. Prior to selecting Go, be sure the printer is on.

42 USING LOTUS 1-2-3

FIGURE 8-3

```
Copyright 1986 Lotus Development Corp.   All Rights Reserved. Release 2.01   MENU
DDDDDDDDDDDDDDDDDDDDDDDDDDDDDDDDDDDDDDDDDDDDDDDDDDDDDDDDDDDDDDDDDDDDDDDDDDDDDDDD
Select graphs for printing
Image-Select  Settings  Go  Align  Page  Exit
MMMMMMMMMMMMMMMMMMMMMMMMMMMMMMMMMMMMMMMMMMMMMMMMMMMMMMMMMMMMMMMMMMMMMMMMMMMMMMMM
        GRAPH          IMAGE OPTIONS                          HARDWARE SETUP
        IMAGES         Size                Range Colors       Graphs Directory:
        SELECTED       Top        .395     X Black              B:\
                       Left       .750     A Black            Fonts Directory:
                       Width     6.500     B Black              A:\
                       Height    4.691     C Black            Interface:
                       Rotate     .000     D Black              Parallel 1
                                           E Black            Printer Type:
                       Font                F Black              IBM GP,Pro/lo
                        1  BLOCK1                             Paper Size
                        2  BLOCK1                               Width       8.500
                                                                Length     11.000

                                                              ACTION OPTIONS
                                                                Pause: No    Eject: No
```

Align: This command resets the top of the page just as /ppa resets the top of the page in the print command of the Lotus System disk.

Page: This command advances the paper in the printer to the top of the page just as /ppp advances the paper in the printer in the print command of the Lotus System disk.

Exit: To exit from the PrintGraph disk, use the Exit option; confirmation will be requested.

9 DATA

In addition to the spreadsheet and graphics functions, Lotus also has database functions. With these functions, you will be able to manipulate the data on your worksheet in many meaningful ways.

Data (referred to as /d), another of the menu options, has several submenu choices. Each of these choices will be examined individually; in addition, the library applications detailed in the second part of this book will utilize a number of these.

A word of advice: save the worksheet before using any of the data commands. It is easy to inadvertently make an error using the data commands; it is usually difficult and time-consuming to reconstruct a worksheet.

Figure 9-1

Fill (referred to as /df): This command numbers a specified range of cells. The cells can be numbered in ascending or descending order. In addition, the user can specify a starting number as well as the increment to be used for subsequent numbers. A blank column or row is used for data fill.

```
FIGURE 9-1

A1:                                                           MENU
Fill  Table  Sort  Query  Distribution  Matrix  Regression  Parse
Fill a range with numbers
         A        B        C        D        E        F        G        H
 1
 2
 3
 4
 5
 6
 7
 8
 9
10
11
12
13
14
15
16
17
18
19
20   Data menu (/d)
24-Mar-88   11:21 AM
```

43

Table (referred to as /dt): This command is useful when attempting to manipulate the values in formulas. The command constructs a table from a formula that has either one or two variables.

Sort (referred to as /ds): This command sorts the records on a worksheet, in either ascending or descending order. To use this command, you must specify a data range and at least a primary sort key. The range to be sorted refers to the portion of the worksheet to be examined by Lotus; often the entire worksheet is the range. The primary sort key is the range by which you want the worksheet to be sorted; a secondary sort key can be specified. After specifying the range and sort key(s), select go (/dsg) and Lotus will perform the sort.

Query (referred to as /dq): This command permits the user to:

1. search a worksheet for particular record(s) using the find option (/dqf)
2. copy all records that match specified criteria using the extract option (/dqe)
3. copy all unique records using the unique option (/dqu) and
4. delete records that match specified criteria using the delete option (/dqd).

Before using these data query commands, you must prepare in several ways. First, you must set up an input range (using /dqi). This tells Lotus which portion of the worksheet is to be searched. The entire worksheet is often selected.

Then, you must set up a criterion range (using /dqc). This range tells Lotus what to search for. The criterion range is placed in an unused portion of the worksheet. It must occupy at least two rows as follows: the first row specifies the column headings as they appear on the worksheet; though not all the column headings need to be copied, as Lotus will only search for those specified in the second row, it may be easier to copy all the column headings using the copy command (/c) in case you decide to search for other fields later. The criteria to be searched is entered on the second row (and any subsequent rows if necessary) directly under the appropriate column headings in the first row of the criterion range.

If you use extract (/dqe) or unique (/dqu), you must also specify an output range (using /dqo); this will tell Lotus where to place the selected records. An unused portion of your worksheet must be selected for the output range. In the top row, specify the column headings you want copied; make sure that the names are exactly the same as those specified in the criterion range, though their order is not important. The output range can be specified as just one row containing the column headings; Lotus will then use as many rows under this specified row as needed. The output range can also be specified as a limited range.

Distribution (referred to as /dd): This selection counts the frequency of the values in the range.

Matrix (referred to as /dm): Square matrices can be inverted; the command also allows multiplication of the matrices.

Regression (referred to as /dr): This command permits regression analysis.

Parse (referred to as /dp): This command is often used when importing a non-Lotus file into Lotus. This option is not available on the earlier versions of Lotus.

10 FORMULAS AND FUNCTIONS

Lotus allows the user to manipulate data with a great number of formulas and functions. Not all of them are appropriate for librarians; only the most useful ones will be discussed here. The Lotus manual lists available formulas and functions. Once you understand the basic ones, the rest can be easily learned as needed.

Since Lotus assumes that all entries beginning with letters are text, all functions and formulas must begin with a 0, 1, 2, 3, 4, 5, 6, 7, 8, 9, ., +, -, (, @, #, or $ (i.e. +A1 can begin a formula). If you simply want to add the contents of two cells, use + the address of the first cell + the address of the second cell (i.e. +A1+A2). To subtract, use + the address of the first cell - the address of the second cell.

If you want to add a column of numbers, you should use a function: all functions begin with @, followed by the name of the function (such as sum), and usually followed by information in parentheses. The function that you would use to add a column or row of numbers is: @SUM(address of first cell..address of last cell). For example, you can add the values of the cells A1 through A20 by using the function @SUM(A1..A20).

Using the @SUM function and the copy command (/c), you can have a running total on your worksheet. If you want a running total of the items in column A, you could use the following in column B:

   B1: @SUM($A$1..A1)

Then, copy cell B1 to the rest of the B column: the first cell address is absolute and will not change when the formula is copied. The second part will change, providing a running total.

In addition to adding and subtracting, Lotus will multiply and divide. To multiply the contents of two cells, place one cell address before and one after a *: the * is the multiplication sign in Lotus. For example, to multiply the contents of cell A1 by the contents of A2, you would write: +A1*A2. Division is simply indicated by using the / between the cell address of the number that you want to divide into and the cell address of the number that you want to divide by. For example, the contents of cell A1 divided by the contents of cell A2 would be written as: +A1/A2.

It should be noted that although cell addresses have been indicated in each case, you can also simply add, subtract, multiply, and divide by any number. Thus, it is possible to multiply the contents of cell A1 by 15: +A1*15.

Sometimes when you have Lotus doing division, you will want to know the remainder in terms of a whole number. To get the remainder, use the function @MOD(the number or cell address of the number being divided into, the number or cell address of the number being divided by). For example, to find the remainder of the division of 25 by 6, you would use the function @MOD(25,6). Lotus will give the answer of 1.

At times, it may be necessary to know the whole number (the integer) of a division. Lotus has a function, @INT(the number or cell address/a number or cell address), that provides this information. Thus, @INT(25/6) reveals 4 as its result.

Furthermore, at times you will want to round a number off to a given number of decimal places. To do this, you would use the @ROUND function: @ROUND(the number or cell address of the number,rounded to the specified number of decimal places). Thus, if you wanted to round the number 1.345 to 1 decimal place, you could use @ROUND(1.345,1). This does not seem to be a very useful function until you realize that it can be combined with other functions and formulas. For example, you can combine the @ROUND function with division: @ROUND(A3/A4,1).

Lotus also has a function that allows an average value to be computed rather easily: @AVG(cell address of the first item on the list..cell address of the last item on the list). This function, combined with an absolute cell address for the first value, permits a running average to be computed just as a running sum was computed above.

On long lists, it might not be easy to locate the maximum and/or minimum values, but Lotus has functions that will do these things for you. The @MAX(cell address of the first item in the list..cell address of the last item in the list) will select the maximum value; @MIN(cell address of the first item in the list..cell address of the last item in the list) will select the minimum value.

A very powerful function is the @IF function. It enables you to have one thing performed if a condition is met, but something else done if the condition is not met. Thus, you can tell Lotus that if the value in cell A1 is equal to 100, do one thing, and if not, do another; instead of equal, you can use > to mean greater than, < to mean less than. In addition, you can combine symbols to produce: <= (meaning less than or equal), >= (meaning greater than or equal), and <> (meaning not equal).

You can also combine terms with logical operators: and, or, and not. These three are always surrounded by # symbols: #and#, #or#, and #not#. These logical operators, as well as the symbols (>,<, etc.), can be used in many functions, but the one most useful to librarians is with @IF.

The format for the @IF function is: @IF(the condition,if the condition is true,if the condition is false). An example of this will illustrate the @IF function:

@IF(A2=100,A1+A2,0)

In other words, if the value of cell A2 is equal to 100 (if the condition is true), add the values of cells A1 and A2 and place the value in this cell; if the value of cell A2 is not equal to 100 (if the condition is false), place a zero in this cell.

Another example may help:

@IF(A2>10#and#A2<20,A1+A2,0)

This complicated expression means that if the value in cell A2 is greater than 10 and less than 20 (between 10 and 20 not including the numbers 10 and 20), add the values in cells A1 and A2 and place that value in the cell in which this function appears; if the value in cell A2 is not greater than 10 and less than 20, place a zero in the cell in which the function appears.

This function, like all the others, can be combined with other functions. Thus the statements in a particular cell can become very complicated:

@IF(@SUM(A2..A20) > (@SUM(B2..B20),@AVG(A2..A20), @AVG(B2..B20)

This complicated statement means that if the sum of the values in cells A2 through A20 is greater than the sum of the values in cells B2 through B20, place the average of the values of the cells from A2 through A20 in the cell that contains the statement; if the sum of the values of cells B2 through B20 is larger (in other words if the condition is false), place the average of the values of cells B2 through B20 in the cell that contains this statement.

For Lotus to perform manipulations on dates, a date function must be used in cells formatted for date. To format for date, use either /wgfd (worksheet global format date) if you want the entire worksheet formatted for date, or /rfd (range format date) to format specific cells or ranges of cells for date. Then, dates must be entered using the date function: @DATE(year,month,date).

These, and other formulas and functions, will be used in the library applications that follow. Illustrations will help to clarify their uses and usefulness.

11 REVIEW

Figure 11-1

To review some of the features of Lotus, construct the following worksheet:
  Some suggestions:
Adjust the column widths for each of the columns. To do this, use /wcs (worksheet column-width set). Date formats usually require at least ten spaces.

Format the first column for date. To do this, use /rfd (range format date); pick any of the date formats.

Format the final column for currency. To do this, use /rfc (range format currency).

To underline the column headings, place the cursor in the beginning of the third line. Type _ (the \ is the code for Lotus to repeat the next character), then depress the return key.

```
FIGURE 11-1

DATABASE SEARCHES: January
Date      Name       Department    DB     Cost
-----------------------------------------------
1/2       Smith      Math          MATH   $37.49
1/2       Jones      Science       CHEM   $42.76
1/4       Jones      Science       CHEM   $4.32
1/4       O'Hara     Art           AHCI   $16.76
1/4       Thomas     Psychology    PSYC   $21.24
1/4       Fried      Math          ERIC   $8.90
1/6       Mann       Science       ERIC   $4.59
1/6       Mann       Science       CHEM   $23.89
1/7       Mann       Science       CHEM   $19.90
1/7       Jones      Science       MAGS   $21.34
1/10      Jones      Science       NOOZ   $4.17
1/10      O'Hara     Art           RELI   $16.76
1/11      Thomas     Psychology    RELI   $19.90
1/11      Fried      Math          NOOZ   $16.78
1/12      Sullivan   Psychology    CRFW   $24.54
1/15      Sell       Nursing       MESH   $2.34
1/15      Smith      Math          PSYC   $5.67
1/16      Jones      Science       PSYC   $2.78
1/18      Smith      Math          ERIC   $1.08
1/20      Thomas     Psychology    PSYC   $23.82
1/24      Hughes     English       LLBA   $19.44
1/26      Hughes     English       ERIC   $2.30
1/27      Smith      Math          ERIC   $4.71
1/27      Smith      Math          MATH   $40.00
1/27      Smith      Math          TSAP   $17.80
1/29      Jones      Science       ERIC   $3.03
1/29      Thomas     Psychology    ERIC   $3.21
1/29      Thomas     Psychology    PSYC   $8.90
1/30      O'Hara     Art           LLBA   $10.11
1/30      Sullivan   Psychology    MESH   $12.09
1/30      Sell       Nursing       NAHL   $14.73
```

The underlining will be repeated across A3. Then use the copy command (/c) to copy cell A3 to cells B3 to E3.

Since the worksheet is longer than one screen, you should use /wth (worksheet titles horizontal) to keep the column headings on screen at all times. Before you use that command, though, place the cursor in the cell below the lines that you want to keep as titles.

Once all the information has been entered, save the worksheet. To save the worksheet, use /fs (file save) and then name the sheet. It is important to save the sheet before you go any further. Now that the worksheet has been saved, we can manipulate it using several of the data commands.

First, number the entries from 1 to 31. To do this, you must first insert a column where you want the numbers to appear (unless you decide to place them in column F). To do the insertion, use /wic (worksheet insert column) and specify where the inserted column is to be placed. Then use the /df (data fill) command. The range is from the top to the end of the A column (which is where the numbers will actually appear). You could have adjusted the column width of this new A column prior to using the data fill command. Specify that you wish to start with 1, use 1 step increments, and end at 31. Depress the enter key, and the numbers will appear in the new A column.

Now, highlight the searches performed for individuals in the Math Department. To do this, you will have to use the /dqf (data query find) command. Specify the input and criterion ranges prior to using /dqf. All the entries with Math in the Department column will be highlighted.

Next, produce a list of all the searches performed in the ERIC database. To do this, you should use the /dqe (data query extract) command. Remember to first set up the input, criterion, and output ranges.

Finally, sort the entire worksheet by name. To do this, use /ds (data sort), specifying the primary sort key as the C (name) column. Similarly, you can sort by department, database, or even cost simply by specifying a different primary sort key.

To practice some of the formulas and functions, add another column to your worksheet, which will produce a running total. To do this, you can write the following in cell G4: @SUM($F$4..F4). Copy this from G4 to the end of the used portion of the worksheet. The $F$4 is an absolute address that anchors that portion of the expression to that cell; the relative F4 changes as the formula is copied, producing a running total.

When you sort the worksheet, do not include the column with the running total in the range specified. It will give you a running total of the newly produced worksheet since its values are determined by the numbers in column F; as these values change, column G is automatically adjusted. Also, when you sort this particular worksheet, do not include column A in the range, which was filled in with the numbers 1 through 31: when you sort, the new sheet will still be numbered correctly.

You can now sort the worksheet by name and then use the @SUM function to produce subtotals by name; the same can be done in terms of department or database. Furthermore, you can determine the percentage spent by department, name, and/or database by dividing the subtotal by the total for the entire sheet.

You can produce a miniature worksheet using /dqe (data query extract); on larger worksheets this would seem more appropriate than using /ds and utilizing only a portion of the sorted worksheet. Be sure to specify the input, criterion, and output ranges prior to /dqe.

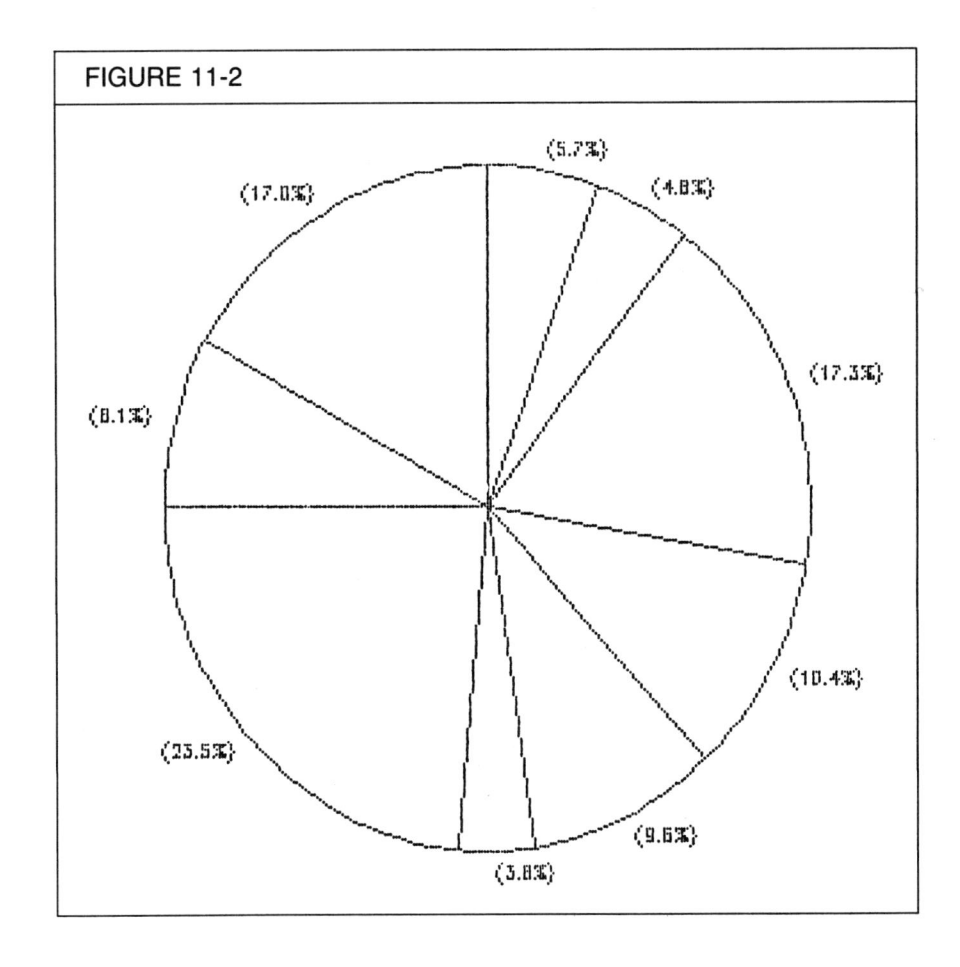

FIGURE 11-2

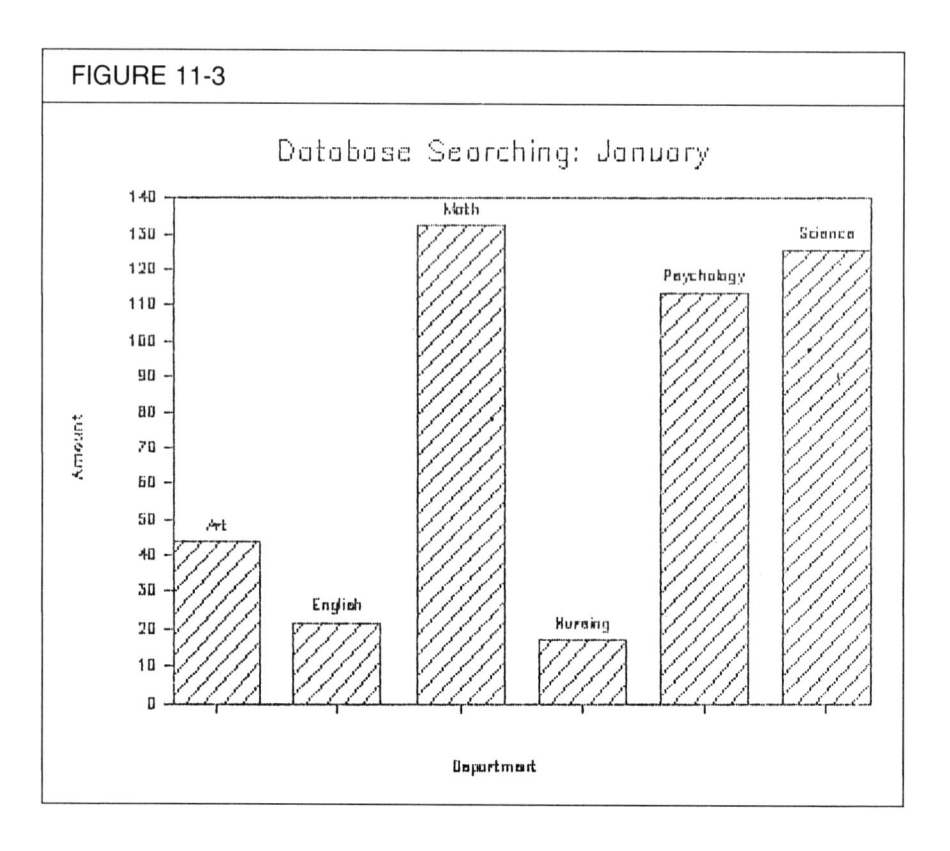

Figure 11-2

GRAPHING

The first type of graph that we will formulate will be a pie chart. The pie chart is actually one of the easiest of the graph options because you only have to specify one range, the A range. Using the worksheet on which you obtained subtotals by either department or name, specify the A range as that column after you have specified the graph type as pie (/gtp). Then simply view the graph if your hardware configuration permits; if not, save the graph and print it by exiting the Lotus System disk and entering the PrintGraph disk. You will notice that Lotus automatically converts the values into percentages, not only showing but actually quantifying how much of the "pie" was spent on each segment. To label each of the slices, you could have added another step to the graphing—specify the X range.

Now, using the same A range, simply change the graph type to bar graph. Then view or print the graph again. Instead of pieces of a pie, you will see bars of different heights for the various values. Lotus sets the scale for you, though the scale can be adjusted. You can add titles, legends, data-labels, etc. to make it all clearer; in the example, blank cells in the columns have been eliminated, and the

FIGURE 11-3

Figure 11-3

appropriate department names have been added to the cells adjacent to the amounts. The options to add data-labels and a title have also been used.

The other types of graphs can be constructed in the same way; be sure to specify the appropriate ranges. If your hardware configuration permits you to view graphs prior to printing them, you can experiment with the settings to see if you have chosen correctly. You can also experiment with the legends, data-labels, etc. to get the most effective presentation.

12 COMMAND SUMMARY

Figure 12-1

Lotus is equipped with a great number of commands; Figure 12-1 details many of those that are available through the menus.

Although some of the commands might seem to overlap in function, they usually do not. A few of the commands that you should be especially sure of not confusing are:

To Erase: /re (range erase) erases the contents of a cell or a range of cells on a given worksheet; if the portion indicated has not been saved, it is lost after this command is executed.

It should be noted that you can also erase the contents of a cell or range of cells by using the copy command (/c) to copy information into an occupied cell: the copied information will replace the information in the cell. You can also use the move command (/m) in the same way: the information in occupied cells is replaced by the new information moved into these cells.

If you simply want to modify the contents of a cell, you can use the edit key, the function key F2. On the other hand, if you want to completely change the contents of a cell, you can simply write over it; the newly written material will replace that which had been in the cell once the enter key is depressed or the highlighter is moved to another cell.

/we (worksheet erase) erases the entire worksheet from the machine's memory; if the worksheet has not been saved onto a disk before this command is executed, the worksheet is lost.

/fe (file erase) erases the file from the disk. If you are working on a file and want to replace the old file with the one you are working on, do not use this command; instead, use /fs (file save) and replace the existing file with the one currently being worked on. The result of this command is permanent.

To delete: To delete columns or rows from a worksheet, use /wdc (worksheet delete column) or /wdr (worksheet delete row).

To insert: To insert either columns or rows, use /wic (worksheet insert column) or /wir (worksheet insert row).

To format cells: There are two separate commands to format cells: one uses /wgf (worksheet global format); the other uses /rf (range format). The format options are substantially identical: the /wgf sets the format for all the cells in the worksheet; the /rf sets the format for a specified range of cells.

FIGURE 12-1

Command	Symbol	Chapter
, (format)	/rf,	2
, (worksheet global format)	/wgf,	1
bar (graph)	/gtb	8
column (worksheet delete)	/wdc	1
column (worksheet insert)	/wic	1
column (worksheet)	/wc	1
combine (file)	/fc	6
copy	/c	3
create (range name)	/rnc	2
currency (format)	/rfc	2
currency (worksheet global format)	/wgfc	1
data	/d	9
date (format)	/rfd	2
date (worksheet global format)	/wgfd	1
delete (range name)	/rnd	2
directory (file)	/fd	6
display (worksheet column)	/wcd	1
distribution (data)	/dd	9
erase (file)	/fe	6
erase (range)	/re	2
erase (worksheet)	/we	1
extract (data query)	/dqe	9
file	/f	6
file (print)	/pf	7
fill (data)	/df	9
find (data query)	/dqf	9
fixed (format)	/rff	2
fixed (worksheet global format)	/wgff	1
format (range)	/rf	2
general (format)	/rfg	2
general (worksheet global format)	/wgfg	1
global format (worksheet)	/wgf	1
graph	/g	8
hidden (format)	/rfh	2
hidden (worksheet global format)	/wgfh	1
hide (worksheet column)	/wch	1
import (file)	/fi	6
input (range)	/ri	2
justify (range)	/rj	2
label prefix (worksheet global)	/wgl	1
label (range)	/rl	2
labels (range name)	/rnl	2
line (graph)	/gtl	8
list (file)	/fl	6
matrix (data)	/dm	9
move	/m	4
name (graph)	/gn	8
options (graph)	/go	8
page (worksheet)	/wp	1
parse (data)	/dp	9
percent (format)	/rfp	2
percent (worksheet global format)	/wgfp	1
pie (graph)	/gtp	8
print	/p	7
printer (print)	/pp	7
protect (range)	/rp	2
protection (worksheet global)	/wgp	1
query (data)	/dq	9
range	/r	2
recalculation (worksheet global)	/wgr	1
regression (data)	/dr	9
reset width (worksheet column)	/wcr	1
reset (format)	/rfr	2
retrieve (file)	/fr	6
row (worksheet delete)	/wdr	1
row (worksheet insert)	/wir	1
save (file)	/fs	6

FIGURE 12-1 *Continued*		
save (graph)	/gs	8
scientific (format)	/rfs	2
scientific (worksheet global format)	/wgfs	1
set width (worksheet column)	/wcs	1
sort (data)	/ds	9
stacked bar (graph)	/gts	8
status (worksheet)	/ws	1
table (data)	/dt	9
table (range name)	/rnt	2
text (format)	/rft	2
text (worksheet global format)	/wgft	1
titles (worksheet)	/wt	1
transpose (range)	/rt	2
type (graph)	/gt	8
unique (data query)	/dqu	9
unprotect (range)	/ru	2
value (range)	/rv	2
view (graph)	/gv	8
window (worksheet)	/ww	1
worksheet	/w	1
xtract (file)	/fx	6
xy (graph)	/gtx	8
zero (worksheet global)	/wgz	1
+/− (format)	/rf+	2
+/− (worksheet global format)	/wgf+	1

To save: There are only two save commands on Lotus: one is used to save a file (/fs), and the other is used to save a graph (/gs).

To restrict changes to cells: /rp (range protect) prohibits changes to specified cells on a worksheet. To permit changes to previously protected cells, use /ru (range unprotect).

/wgp (worksheet global protect) protects the entire worksheet from changes. This command can be used in conjunction with /ru (range unprotect) to unprotect a limited number of cells or ranges. On a large worksheet, this technique may save time.

/ri (range input) protects ranges of cells by not allowing the cursor to be moved to specified portions of the worksheet.

/wch (worksheet column hide) conceals columns of the worksheet from the user's view. To display formerly hidden cells, use /wcd (worksheet column display). These commands are only available on the more recent releases of Lotus.

/rfh (range format hidden) conceals the contents of specified cells from the user's view. To view the contents of previously hidden cells, use /rfd (range format display). These commands are only available on the more recent releases of Lotus.

13 MACROS

Lotus allows a streamlining of some of the commands and repetitive keystroking through the use of macros. A macro is a set of instructions to Lotus which is made up of a series of keystrokes.

Macros must be written in a blank area of a worksheet. If a macro line begins with a nontext character, a label prefix must be added to precede it. Any label prefix will do, though ' is usually used. Lotus automatically adds a label prefix (by changing from the ready mode to the label mode) to lines beginning with characters other than the numbers 0 through 9, as well as the following characters: + - . (@ / # and $; if a macro line begins with a character other than one of those listed, a label prefix need not be included. On the other hand, if a macro line begins with one of these characters, a label prefix must be added so that Lotus will enter the information in the label, rather than the value, mode. Macros can use any of the keys on a keyboard plus any of the special keys. Though a macro can be more than one cell long, only the first cell address has to be specified when the macro is named (using the range name create command: /rnc): Lotus reads down a column of macro commands until it reaches a blank cell. Then it stops. Thus, a macro must be followed by a blank cell.

A macro must be named, using the /rnc (range name create) command. A macro must be named beginning with the \ followed by one letter or the 0 (zero).

To use (called invoke) a named macro, depress the macro key (which in many cases is the key marked ALT) and the letter portion of the macro name: you can consider the ALT as substituting for the \. Lotus will then execute the macro.

If you have a certain set of commands that you want to be executed every time you retrieve a worksheet, you should name the macro \0: this is the auto-execute macro name. It cannot be invoked manually by depressing the macro key and 0.

After you have written a macro, you may find that you have to edit it: a macro can be edited like any other cell with the edit key, the function key F2. Simply make the necessary corrections. If your macro is complicated, you can use the STEP mode, which performs the macro in a step-by-step fashion, awaiting your input before proceeding to the next step. With the STEP mode, you can edit each step as it appears. To invoke the STEP mode, depress the step key (ALT and F1 in release 1A; ALT and F2 in later releases of Lotus). When in the STEP mode, SST will flash at the bottom of the display.

It is also possible to have an interactive macro: in an interactive macro, Lotus will perform the macro as written until it gets to a {?}. At that point, Lotus will pause and wait for input from the user.

Then Lotus will continue the macro. The interactive feature has been used, for example, in macros that perform data sorts, to enable the user to specify the primary and/or secondary sort key(s).

A list of the special key possibilities and macro keywords is included in the Lotus manual, and it is available through the online help facility (depress the function key F1, get the help menu, and choose macros). All special key possibilities are enclosed in braces, such as {RIGHT}; the only exception to this rule is the ~, which represents the enter key.

To write a macro, you should manually go through all the steps involved in the process, writing down each and every keystroke, including the use of the enter key. When you are certain that you have noted all the keystrokes necessary, find a blank portion of the worksheet and start; then name and invoke the macro. If it works, save the worksheet (with the macro); if not, edit the macro and try it again. It is helpful to name ranges in your worksheet: this makes specifying ranges in the macro easier.

You should get into the habit of protecting the cells that contain macros; this will prevent users from inadvertently tampering with the macro that you have constructed. To protect a cell or range of cells, you can use /rp (range protect); you can also use /ri (range input), which will prevent the cursor from being moved to the indicated portion of the worksheet. On the more recent releases of Lotus you can also use /wch (worksheet column hide), which will keep the column(s) with the macro(s) hidden from the view of the user.

Below are a few examples of macros; more will be shown in the library applications in the second part of this work.

INSERT COLUMN OR ROW

A simple macro to insert a column: though this macro does not save very much time, it is useful in illustrating what a macro can do:

'/WIC~

Symbol	Meaning
'	Label prefix
/	Calls up the Lotus menu
WIC	Worksheet Insert Column
	Return: if the cursor is placed in the column which you want to be a blank column, the return is all that is needed

If you want to write a macro to insert a row instead of a column, simply modify the above macro as follows: '/WIR~ (the R stands for row where the C stood for column).

INTERACTIVE SORT MACRO

This macro is useful on worksheets that you frequently sort using different primary sort keys:

'/DSD{HOME}{END}{DOWN}{END}{RIGHT}~P{?}~A~G~

This macro might look very complicated until you look at it one step at a time:

Symbol	Meaning
'	Label prefix
/DSD	Menu Data Sort Data-Range: at this point, Lotus automatically places the user in the point mode
{HOME}	Moves the cursor to the home position
{END}{DOWN}	Highlights the first column by moving the cursor to the last occupied row in column A
{END}{RIGHT}	Highlights the entire worksheet by moving the cursor to the last occupied column on the worksheet
~	Enter
P	Primary sort key
{?}	This symbol instructs Lotus to pause for user input: the user defines the primary sort key before Lotus continues
~A~G~	Return, Ascending (in response to the prompt about the order in which the primary key should be sorted), and finally go ahead and sort, and a return

You could edit this macro to include an interactive secondary sort key by adding ~S{?}~A after the first {?}.

If you are using a recent release of Lotus, you can add {BEEP} directly before the {?}: this will tell Lotus to sound a beep where the user input is necessary.

It should be noted that this macro will only work if the entire first column and last row are filled; otherwise, the {END}{DOWN} and {END}{RIGHT} will not work properly.

PRINT MACRO

The following print macro can be used to print the entire worksheet, move the paper in the printer to the top of the page, and return to the worksheet by quitting the print menu:

'/PPR{HOME}.{END}{DOWN}{END}{RIGHT}GPQ

Symbol	Meaning
'	Label prefix
/PPR	Menu Print Printer Range
{HOME}	Moves the cursor to the home position
.{END}{DOWN}	Places Lotus in the point mode, then highlights the first column
{END}{RIGHT}	Highlights the entire worksheet
G	Tells Lotus to go ahead and print
P	Advances the paper in the printer to the top of the next page after the printing has been completed
Q	Quits the print menu and returns the user to the worksheet

Due to the functioning of the end key, this macro is only possible when using a worksheet that does not contain blank cells in the first column as well as in the last row.

REPLACE FILE AND EXIT LOTUS

A macro that can be used to replace an existing file with updated information and then automatically exit Lotus to the opening screen follows:

'/FS~R/QY

Symbol	Meaning
'	Label prefix
/FS	Menu File Save
~R	Enter Replace the existing file with the new file
/QY	Menu Quit Yes (end current session)

At this point you will be able to end the Lotus session completely or proceed to the PrintGraph disk.

GRAPH: PIE CHARTS

A pie chart is one of the simplest graphs to create. An interactive macro for creating pie charts is:

'/GTPA{?}~S{?}~Q

Symbol	Meaning
'	Label prefix
/GTP	Graph Type Pie
A	A range; the only required range for pie charts
{?}	Tells Lotus to pause for user input: in this case a range must be specified for the pie chart
~S	Enter Save
{?}	Tells Lotus to pause for user input: in this case, the name under which this graph should be saved
~Q	Enter Quit: returns the user to the worksheet

A further enhancement: if your hardware configuration permits you to view graphs, you should add V{?} after the pause for the A range specification. If the graph does not look as you wish, you can terminate the macro by depressing the escape key several times.

If you are using a recent release of Lotus, you can further refine your macro by inserting {BEEP} before each {?}: this will tell Lotus to signal the user that input is required.

If you are interested in constructing bar graphs rather than pie charts, you can modify the macro's beginning to be: '/gtb (graph type bar). The rest of the macro remains the same.

It should be noted that as the macro is currently written, no legends, titles, or data-labels are produced: further interactive steps can be introduced into the macro to permit the insertion of these enhancements. For example, with the pie chart, after the A range has been specified, you could add X{?} or (in the later releases of Lotus) X{BEEP}{?} to ask for the X range specifications. In the pie chart, the X range acts as labels for each of the slices.

Numerous macros are used in the library applications that follow; each is fully explained as it is used.

PART II

LIBRARY APPLICATIONS

INTRODUCTION

Each of the chapters in this section applies the commands, formulas, and functions described in the first section. Numerous macros are also utilized.

The applications are arranged to proceed from the simple to more complex uses of Lotus in library related situations. At the beginning of each application, reference is given to the chapters from the first section that discuss the commands, formulas, and functions being applied.

Though suggestions for modifications are provided throughout, each of the applications can be used exactly as given. The modifications will help to customize these applications to a particular library situation. Further modifications are suggested to permit the use of any release of Lotus with each of the applications.

14 DEPARTMENT BUDGET

PROBLEM
I want to keep track of the budget for one particular department. While keeping track of the expenditures, I want to know how much of my budget has been spent as well as how much remains to be encumbered.

COMMANDS
Copy (/c: chapter 3)
Data distribution (/dd: chapter 9)
Data query find (/dqf: chapter 9)
Graph (/g: chapter: 8)
Range format currency (/rfc: chapter 2)
Range format date (/rfd: chapter 2)
Worksheet column-width set (/wcs: chapter 1)
Worksheet titles horizontal (/wth: chapter 1).

FUNCTIONS
@DATE and @SUM (chapter 10).

CONCEPTS
Absolute and relative cell addresses (chapter 3).

Figure 14-1

A nine-column worksheet can be used to keep track of the expenditures of a department; each of the columns will be discussed separately.

Column A, date, records the date on which an order was placed. This column should be formatted for date (/rfd: range format date), and the column width should be adjusted to accommodate the format chosen (/wcs: worksheet column-width set). When entering dates in this column of the worksheet, it is important to use the @DATE function; this will permit you to do date calculations.

Column B, vendor, records the name of the vendor with whom the order has been placed. If you wish, you can use an extra column to record the vendor's address, though this is not always important. You must adjust the column width (/wcs: worksheet column-width set) of this column to accommodate vendors' names: a width of at least 20 is necessary.

Column C, approximate bill, records the approximate amount to be billed. This number will be used to compute the approximate amount left in the budget of the department. This column should be formatted for currency (/rfc: range format currency) with two decimal places (for cents). The column width should also be adjusted if you believe that the amount will occupy more than nine spaces (use /wcs: worksheet column-width set to adjust the column width).

Column D, approximate remaining, records the approximate amount remaining in the budget by subtracting the approximate bill (column C) from the budget amount remaining. If the total budget amount were $12,000.00, the formula in cell D4 would be +12000-C4, with C4 being the approximate amount of the first order placed. In cell D5, the formula would be +D4-C5; when this formula is copied (using the copy command, /c), Lotus will automatically adjust the cell addresses to provide a running approximate total remaining since the cell addresses are relative. This column should be formatted for currency (/rfc: range format currency) with two decimal places. If a wider column is needed for the budget, use /wcs (worksheet column-width set) to set the column width.

Columns E and F are used for the date the merchandise and invoice are received. Often these two do not arrrive at the same time, and it is often necessary to document when each was received. Since these columns are used for recording dates, they should each be formatted for date (/rfd: range format date), and the column widths should be adjusted (/wcs: worksheet column-width set) for the format selected. Enter dates using the @DATE function.

Column G, amount paid, records the actual amount paid for the

68 USING LOTUS 1-2-3

```
FIGURE 14-1

A1: [W15]                                                           READY

              A              B              C              D
   1
   2  Date           Vender         Approx Bill    Approx Remain
   3  ------------------------------------------------------------------
   4                                              12000-C4
   5                                              +D4-C5
   6                                              +D5-C6
   7                                              +D6-C7
   8                                              +D7-C8
   9                                              +D8-C9
  10                                              +D9-C10
  11                                              +D10-C11
  12                                              +D11-C12
  13                                              +D12-C13
  14                                              +D13-C14
  15                                              +D14-C15
  16                                              +D15-C16
  17                                              +D16-C17
  18                                              +D17-C18
  19                                              +D18-C19
  20                                              +D19-C20
  30-Nov-88  10:23 AM
```

ordered item. At times this amount will differ from the approximate bill and cause the approximate amount remaining to be different from the amount remaining. This difference can be caused partially by items being out of stock, etc. This column should be formatted for currency (/rfc: range format currency) with two decimal places. The column width may have to be adjusted according to the size of the budget (use /wcs, worksheet column-width set, to adjust the width of the column if necessary).

Column H, total spent, records the actual total spent by providing a running total of the amounts from column G, amount paid. Thus, in cell H4, the amount from G4 is simply copied since it is the first amount spent. This is accomplished by using +G4 in cell H4. In cell H5, the amount from G5 is added to the previous balance (from the cell above) using the formula +H4+G5. By leaving the cell addresses relative, you can use the copy com-

DEPARTMENT BUDGET **69**

Figure 14-2

mand (/c) to fill in the formula for the entire column. Lotus will automatically adjust the relative cell addresses as it copies the formula.

Alternatively, you can compute the total spent in Column H using a different formula:

$$@SUM(\$G\$4..G4)$$

Figure 14-3

When this formula is copied down column H using the copy command (/c), the first cell address will not change since it is absolute (because of the dollar signs); the second cell address will automatically be adjusted, as it is a relative address.

Column I, total remaining, is similar to column D, except that it records the actual amount remaining in the budget rather than the approximate amount not encumbered. This column subtracts the

---

```
FIGURE 14-2

E1: [W12]                                                           READY


           E           F           G           H
  1
  2    Inv Rec'd    Item rec'd  Amt. Paid   Total Spent   Total Remain
  3    ------------------------------------------------------------
  4                                         +G4           12000-G4
  5                                         +G5+H4        +I4-G5
  6                                         +G6+H5        +I5-G6
  7                                         +G7+H6        +I6-G7
  8                                         +G8+H7        +I7-G8
  9                                         +G9+H8        +I8-G9
 10                                         +G10+H9       +I9-G10
 11                                         +G11+H10      +I10-G11
 12                                         +G12+H11      +I11-G12
 13                                         +G13+H12      +I12-G13
 14                                         +G14+H13      +I13-G14
 15                                         +G15+H14      +I14-G15
 16                                         +G16+H15      +I15-G16
 17                                         +G17+H16      +I16-G17
 18                                         +G18+H17      +I17-G18
 19                                         +G19+H18      +I18-G19
 20                                         +G20+H19      +I19-G20
25-Mar-88   11:18 AM
```

70 USING LOTUS 1-2-3

FIGURE 14-3

```
E1: [W12]                                                          READY


            E          F           G            H
 1
 2    Inv Rec'd   Item rec'd  Amt. Paid    Total Spent   Total Remain
 3    ---------------------------------------------------------------
 4                                         @SUM($G$4..G4)  12000-G4
 5                                         @SUM($G$4..G5)  +I4-G5
 6                                         @SUM($G$4..G6)  +I5-G6
 7                                         @SUM($G$4..G7)  +I6-G7
 8                                         @SUM($G$4..G8)  +I7-G8
 9                                         @SUM($G$4..G9)  +I8-G9
10                                         @SUM($G$4..G10) +I9-G10
11                                         @SUM($G$4..G11) +I10-G11
12                                         @SUM($G$4..G12) +I11-G12
13                                         @SUM($G$4..G13) +I12-G13
14                                         @SUM($G$4..G14) +I13-G14
15                                         @SUM($G$4..G15) +I14-G15
16                                         @SUM($G$4..G16) +I15-G16
17                                         @SUM($G$4..G17) +I16-G17
18                                         @SUM($G$4..G18) +I17-G18
19                                         @SUM($G$4..G19) +I18-G19
20                                         @SUM($G$4..G20) +I19-G20
25-Mar-88   11:20 AM
```

Figure 14-4

total spent from the total amount of the budget. This is accomplished using the formula +12000-G4 in cell I4, assuming that the total department budget is $12,000. Cell G4 contains the amount paid for the first listed purchase. In cell I5, the formula +I4-G5 is used to subtract the spent amount from the amount of the budget remaining. This formula is copied down the I column using the copy command (/c), and Lotus automatically changes the relative cell addresses to provide a running balance.

Alternatively, you can use a different formula for this column: +12000-H4, where cell H4 contains the total amount spent. When this is copied down the column, a running total is provided because the cell address of H4 is relative.

No matter which of the formulas is used to obtain the total remaining, this column should be formatted for currency (/rfc: range format currency) with two decimal places. If necessary, the column width should be adjusted (/wcs: worksheet column-width set).

FIGURE 14-4

```
F1:                                                              READY


              F           G            H             I
 1
 2    Item rec'd     Amt. Paid    Total Spent   Total Remain
 3    ----------------------------------------------------------------
 4                                @SUM($G$4..G4)  12000-H4
 5                                @SUM($G$4..G5)  12000-H5
 6                                @SUM($G$4..G6)  12000-H6
 7                                @SUM($G$4..G7)  12000-H7
 8                                @SUM($G$4..G8)  12000-H8
 9                                @SUM($G$4..G9)  12000-H9
10                                @SUM($G$4..G10) 12000-H10
11                                @SUM($G$4..G11) 12000-H11
12                                @SUM($G$4..G12) 12000-H12
13                                @SUM($G$4..G13) 12000-H13
14                                @SUM($G$4..G14) 12000-H14
15                                @SUM($G$4..G15) 12000-H15
16                                @SUM($G$4..G16) 12000-H16
17                                @SUM($G$4..G17) 12000-H17
18                                @SUM($G$4..G18) 12000-H18
19                                @SUM($G$4..G19) 12000-H19
20                                @SUM($G$4..G20) 12000-H20
30-Nov-88   10:24 AM
```

To make the worksheet look better, you can underline the column headings using _ in column A; the \ tells Lotus to repeat the following character for the entire cell when the enter key is depressed. The copy command (/c) is then used to copy the underlining to each of the remaining 8 cells that contain the column headings.

Lotus can then be told to keep the column headings on screen even if the screen scrolls up to accommodate more than the number of lines that can be seen on a screen at one time. This is done by using the titles command (/wth: worksheet title horizontal); the cursor must be in the cell under the underlining in the A column when this command is used in order to keep the titles and underlining on screen.

USING THE WORKSHEET

When using a long worksheet, you may find it hard to locate a particular order. Rather than examining each record individually, you can use the data query find command (/dqf: data query find) to locate a particular record (in this case, you may need to locate a particular vendor). This command will highlight each of the records that match the criterion that you have chosen.

In order for Lotus to do this highlighting, you must specify both input and criterion ranges. The input range tells Lotus where to look for the matching records; the criterion range tells Lotus exactly what to look for. For the department budget worksheet, you will probably want to use the entire worksheet as the input range. The criterion should contain the column headings that will be searched for (on the first line) as well as what is to be searched for (on the second line). You do not need to have all the column headings listed on the first line of the criterion range, but it doesn't hurt to do this, since you may want to have Lotus highlight records that match criterion from any one or several of the columns. In addition, it is easy to use the copy command to copy the column headings to the criterion range: use /c, highlight the column headings, depress enter, move the cursor to a blank portion of the worksheet (in this case a few columns to the right works well), and then depress the enter key. On the second line of the criterion range, under the appropriate heading, indicate what Lotus is to find. More than one column can be used. Lotus will then only select those records which match all of the indicated criteria.

Finally, select data query find (/dqf). The first record that matches the indicated criterion will be highlighted. Using the arrow keys, subsequent records that match the specified criterion will be highlighted.

Another data command that you may want to use on your worksheet is data distribution (/dd). This command counts the number of records that fall within certain specified limits. In the case of this worksheet, you may want to find out how many of the orders cost under $300, between $300 and $600, and over $600. Of course, these numbers can be changed, and any number of these values can be specified.

To perform a data distribution (/dd), you will be asked to specify a values range, which is the column from which Lotus is to count. In the sample, the amount paid column would be indicated. Lotus then requests a bin range, which is the column with the values to be counted. The bin range must be set up before the data distribution is begun. In the sample, the following numbers would be placed in one column outside of the used portion of the worksheet with a blank row next to it for Lotus to record the frequencies: 300 and 600. These numbers must be in ascending order; otherwise the results will be unreliable. These cells would be indicated as the bin range, and when /dd (data distribution) is invoked, Lotus will record the distributions, first of those records with values between 0 and $300, then $301 to $600, and finally over $600.

These values can then be graphed: a bar graph would probably be effective (/gtb), using the bin range as the X range and the frequency as the A range.

15 BOOK BUDGET

PROBLEM
I want to keep track of the book budget for the entire library; I need to know how much is spent for materials for each of the collections, including serials, reference, and the general circulating collection. In addition, I need to have an idea of the total amount spent, as well as the amount remaining in the budget.

COMMANDS
Copy (/c: chapter 3)
Range format date (/rfd: chapter 2)
Worksheet global column-width set (/wgcs: chapter 1)
Worksheet global format currency (/wgfc: chapter 1).

FORMULAS AND FUNCTIONS
Addition, subtraction and @SUM (chapter 10).

CONCEPTS
Relative and mixed cell addresses (chapter 3).

To solve this problem, set up a worksheet which contains two columns for each of the collections to be monitored: one column for the amount of each purchase for the collection and the other for total spent by collection. In the sample worksheet, there are two special collections as well as reference, serials, and the circulating collection. In addition, there is one column for the date, one for the total spent, and one for the amount remaining in the budget.

To begin, format the entire worksheet for currency with two decimal places (/wgfc2: worksheet global format currency 2 decimal places). Using a global formating will save you time, since all the columns need to be formatted in this way except for the date column. After the global formatting, format the date column for date (/rfd: range format date), which will override the global command for this range only.

Then, adjust the column widths for all the columns using /wgcs (worksheet global column-width set): the date format that you have chosen will probably require more than 9 as the column width, and so will the other columns, depending on how large the budget is.

Each of the columns used for the total spent on individual collections or departments will utilize a similar function:

@SUM(c$4..c4)

This formula is then copied (/c) down the column, and because the first cell address is mixed, the first row reference will not change.

FIGURE 15-1

```
LIBRARY BOOK BUDGET
Total Budget=$100,000
Date         Reference      REF TOTAL         Serials       SER TOTAL         Sp Coll 1      SP TOTAL
                            @SUM(B$4..B4)                   @SUM(D$4..D4)                    @SUM(F$4..F4)
                            @SUM(B$4..B5)                   @SUM(D$4..D5)                    @SUM(F$4..F5)
                            @SUM(B$4..B6)                   @SUM(D$4..D6)                    @SUM(F$4..F6)
                            @SUM(B$4..B7)                   @SUM(D$4..D7)                    @SUM(F$4..F7)
                            @SUM(B$4..B8)                   @SUM(D$4..D8)                    @SUM(F$4..F8)
                            @SUM(B$4..B9)                   @SUM(D$4..D9)                    @SUM(F$4..F9)
                            @SUM(B$4..B10)                  @SUM(D$4..D10)                   @SUM(F$4..F10)
                            @SUM(B$4..B11)                  @SUM(D$4..D11)                   @SUM(F$4..F11)
                            @SUM(B$4..B12)                  @SUM(D$4..D12)                   @SUM(F$4..F12)
                            @SUM(B$4..B13)                  @SUM(D$4..D13)                   @SUM(F$4..F13)
                            @SUM(B$4..B14)                  @SUM(D$4..D14)                   @SUM(F$4..F14)
                            @SUM(B$4..B15)                  @SUM(D$4..D15)                   @SUM(F$4..F15)
```

Continued

Since the second cell address is relative, it will automatically be adjusted by Lotus as it is copied, thus providing a running total.

The above formula can then be copied across the worksheet for each of the columns for total by collection or department. Since the first cell address is mixed and the second is relative, when the formula is copied across the worksheet using the copy command (/c), only the column references will be changed. Then the formula can in turn be copied down each of the remaining columns using the copy command (/c), and Lotus again adjusts the second cell address automatically.

The column in which the total spent is recorded simply adds the values in the cells from the total by department or collection along that line. This is accomplished using the formula:

+C4+E4+G4+I4+K4

This formula is also copied (/c) down the column, and because none of the cell addresses is absolute or mixed, Lotus will automatically adjust each of them.

Finally, the last column subtracts the total spent from the total book budget. In the example, the total book budget is $100,000, and the formula is:

100000-L4

Column L contains the total spent by all the departments. This

---

FIGURE 15-1 *Continued*

Sp Coll 2	SP TOTAL	Circ	CIRC TOTAL	Total	Remaining
	@SUM(H$4..H4)		@SUM(J$4..J4)	+C4+E4+G4+I4+K4	100000-L4
	@SUM(H$4..H5)		@SUM(J$4..J5)	+C5+E5+G5+I5+K5	100000-L5
	@SUM(H$4..H6)		@SUM(J$4..J6)	+C6+E6+G6+I6+K6	100000-L6
	@SUM(H$4..H7)		@SUM(J$4..J7)	+C7+E7+G7+I7+K7	100000-L7
	@SUM(H$4..H8)		@SUM(J$4..J8)	+C8+E8+G8+I8+K8	100000-L8
	@SUM(H$4..H9)		@SUM(J$4..J9)	+C9+E9+G9+I9+K9	100000-L9
	@SUM(H$4..H10)		@SUM(J$4..J10)	+C10+E10+G10+I10+K10	100000-L10
	@SUM(H$4..H11)		@SUM(J$4..J11)	+C11+E11+G11+I11+K11	100000-L11
	@SUM(H$4..H12)		@SUM(J$4..J12)	+C12+E12+G12+I12+K12	100000-L12
	@SUM(H$4..H13)		@SUM(J$4..J13)	+C13+E13+G13+I13+K13	100000-L13
	@SUM(H$4..H14)		@SUM(J$4..J14)	+C14+E14+G14+I14+K14	100000-L14
	@SUM(H$4..H15)		@SUM(J$4..J15)	+C15+E15+G15+I15+K15	100000-L15

Worksheet printed using Sideways

Figure 15-1

formula is also copied (/c), and Lotus automatically adjusts the cell address.

You may want to graph the results of this worksheet using a pie chart. Each of the amounts spent by the departments will become a slice of the pie. Use /gtp (graph type pie chart) to indicate pie chart, and then the A range will be the total for each department, and the X range will be the column headings.

16 LIBRARY BUDGET

PROBLEM
The budget for my library is set, but costs keep going up. Salaries as well as supplies and expenses are increasing in cost, cutting into the library materials budget. Is there a way that I can easily show the board of directors the effect of different percentages of increases in each of these areas on the purchase of library materials?

COMMANDS
Data table (/dt: chapter 9)
Worksheet global format currency (/wgfc: chapter 1).

FORMULAS
Addition, subtraction, and multiplication (chapter 10).

Lotus provides the data table command (/dt) to find out the effect of "what if" situations. In this case, it will determine the effect that a varying percent increase in salaries as well as a separate varying increase in the cost of supplies and expenses will have on the library's ability to purchase library materials.

Since there are two variables involved in this case, data table 2 is selected (/dt2). Before selecting this menu choice, though, you must set up your worksheet.

First format the entire worksheet for currency (/wgfc) with two decimal places. Cell A1, whose column width should be adjusted (/wcs20: worksheet column-width set 20) to accommodate the title of the worksheet: Library Budget. The total budget should be placed in the adjacent cell (B1); in this case it is $150,000.

Then, the heading Salaries was placed in cell A2, Supplies and Expenses in cell A3, and Library Materials in cell A4. Hypothetical values were placed adjacent to each of these: B2: $75,000, B3: $10,000, and B4: $65,000.

Then the table was created by detailing the possible percentage of increases in salaries across the top row of an unused portion of a worksheet: increases from a low of 2% to a high of 5.5%, with .5% steps were placed. By using the formula +B2*1.02 (cell B2 contains the current amount the library spends on salaries, * is the Lotus symbol for multiplication, and 1.02 indicates 102%, or an increase of 2%). This formula was modified for each of the possible percentage increases along the row.

The first column of the data table, which is one column to the left of the first percentage increase, was used to record increases in the

FIGURE 16-1

```
LIBRARY BUDGET         $150,000.00
Salaries                $75,000.00
Supplies, Equipment     $10,000.00
Library Materials       $65,000.00

                +B1-(B2+B3)    1.02*B2       1.025*B2      1.03*B2       1.035*B2
                +$B$3*1.02     $63,300.00    $62,925.00    $62,550.00    $62,175.00
                +$B$3*1.025    $63,250.00    $62,875.00    $62,500.00    $62,125.00
                +$B$3*1.03     $63,200.00    $62,825.00    $62,450.00    $62,075.00
                +$B$3*1.035    $63,150.00    $62,775.00    $62,400.00    $62,025.00
                +$B$3*1.04     $63,100.00    $62,725.00    $62,350.00    $61,975.00
                +$B$3*1.045    $63,050.00    $62,675.00    $62,300.00    $61,925.00
                +$B$3*1.05     $63,000.00    $62,625.00    $62,250.00    $61,875.00
                +$B$3*1.055    $62,950.00    $62,575.00    $62,200.00    $61,825.00
                +$B$3*1.06     $62,900.00    $62,525.00    $62,150.00    $61,775.00
                +$B$3*1.065    $62,850.00    $62,475.00    $62,100.00    $61,725.00
                +$B$3*1.07     $62,800.00    $62,425.00    $62,050.00    $61,675.00
```

Continued

cost of supplies and expenses. These increases were also in .5% steps, starting at 2% and going as high as 7%. The formula +B3*1.02 was utilized (cell B3 contains the amount currently spent on supplies and expenses, * is the Lotus symbol for multiplication, and 1.02 indicates an increase of 2%).

The blank cell at the top left hand corner of the table is filled in with the formula which Lotus will use to compute the data table. In this case, since the total library budget minus the salaries and the supplies and expenses will equal the amount to be spent on library materials, the formula +B1-(B2+B3) is placed here.

You are now ready to invoke the data table command: /dt2, since there are two variables. The table range is the entire table, including the values already in place as well as the blank cells which Lotus will fill in. The first and second input ranges are cells into which Lotus will insert each of the values from the table into the formula: in this case two blank cells were specified (C2 and C3). Lotus indicates that you should wait, and in a short while the table is filled in, revealing the effects of different salary and supplies and expenses increases on the ability of the library to purchase library materials.

Figure 16-1

If you decide to change the values in either the column or row indicating percentage increases, or you decide to change the formula or the values in cells B1, B2, B3 or B4, you can simply change them and then depress the function key F8. All of the previously indicated variables are used to recalculate the data table.

FIGURE 16-1 Continued

1.04*B2	1.045*B2	1.05*B2	1.055*B2
$61,800.00	$61,425.00	$61,050.00	$60,675.00
$61,750.00	$61,375.00	$61,000.00	$60,625.00
$61,700.00	$61,325.00	$60,950.00	$60,575.00
$61,650.00	$61,275.00	$60,900.00	$60,525.00
$61,600.00	$61,225.00	$60,850.00	$60,475.00
$61,550.00	$61,175.00	$60,800.00	$60,425.00
$61,500.00	$61,125.00	$60,750.00	$60,375.00
$61,450.00	$61,075.00	$60,700.00	$60,325.00
$61,400.00	$61,025.00	$60,650.00	$60,275.00
$61,350.00	$60,975.00	$60,600.00	$60,225.00
$61,300.00	$60,925.00	$60,550.00	$60,175.00

Worksheet printed using Sideways

17 BUDGET REQUEST

PROBLEM
I would like to simplify my budget requests. Can Lotus help?

COMMANDS
Copy (/c: chapter 3)
Graph type pie chart (/gtp: chapter 8)
Range format currency (/rfc: chapter 2)
Range format percent (/rfp: chapter 2)
Worksheet column-width set (/wcs: chapter 1).

FUNCTIONS
@SUM (chapter 10).

CONCEPTS
Absolute and relative cell addresses (chapter 3).

Figure 17-1

The key to a budget request worksheet is the function that adds the values in a specified range: @SUM(range). This function is used several times in the worksheet.

The A column of the worksheet should be widened to accommodate the budget line headings: a width of 25 should be sufficient. To widen the column, use /wcs25 (worksheet column-width 25).

The B column should be formatted for currency, using /rfc2 (range format currency with two decimal places).

The first cell (A1) is used for the title of the worksheet: LIBRARY BUDGET REQUEST, and this line is double underlined by placing the cursor in cell A2, depressing the \, and then the =. When the enter key is depressed, the = sign is repeated for the entire length of the cell because \ is the repeat signal for Lotus.

In the sample worksheet, the library budget request is divided into five sections: Salaries and Wages, Supplies and Expenses, Equipment, Books and Materials, and Other. Under each of the headings, specific items are given their own lines. (For example, the first heading, Salaries and Wages, is subdivided into separate lines for: Professionals, Library Technical Assistants, Clericals, Temporary Services/Hourly, and Other/Miscellaneous.) Totals are provided for each of the headings. Lotus adds the values from each of the lines in the heading to provide a total for that portion of the budget by using the @SUM function. From the example, the total for Salaries and Wages is provided by using the function:

@SUM(b6..b10)

This function is placed in the cell next to the category heading, providing a total for the category.

You can use this worksheet for a multiple year budget request: simply add columns, one for each year. You can even add extra columns in which you have Lotus compute the percentage change from one year to the next. The columns used for the amount of the request should be formatted for currency (/rfc) with two decimal places. The columns used for percents should be formatted for percent (/rfp).

GRAPHING
If you want to present the information in graph form, a pie chart would probably be most effective. To create a pie chart, copy each of the totals and category headings to an unused portion of the worksheet. You will not be able to use the copy command (/c) for this because, if you do, Lotus will automatically adjust the ranges inside the functions unless you made each of the cell addresses

FIGURE 17-1

```
                        LIBRARY BUDGET
                        ==============================

                        Salaries and Wages          $0.00
                        ------------------------------
                        Professionals
                        LTA
                        Clericals
                        Temp Service/Hourly
                        Other/Misc

                        Supplies and Expenses       $0.00
                        ------------------------------
                        Supplies
                        Communication
                        Stationery
                        Utilities
                        Contractual Services
                        Other/Misc

                        Equipment                   $0.00
                        ------------------------------
                        Furniture
                        Motor vehicle
                        AV
                        Computers/Terminals
                        Other/Misc

                        Books & Materials           $0.00
                        ------------------------------
                        Books
                        Serials
                        AV/Microforms
                        Binding
                        Services
                        Other/Misc

                        Other                       $0.00
                        ------------------------------
                        Building and Repair
                        Local Travel
                        Out of town travel
                        Contingency
                        Other/Misc

                        Total Budget:               $0.00



                        Salaries and Wages          $0.00
                        Supplies and Expenses       $0.00
                        Equipment                   $0.00
                        Books & Materials           $0.00
                        Other                       $0.00
```

Continued

FIGURE 17-1 *Continued*

```
A1: [W30] 'LIBRARY BUDGET                                                READY


                   A                        B              C         D
1    LIBRARY BUDGET
2    =====================================
3
4    Salaries and Wages          @SUM(B6..B10)
5    -------------------------------------
6    Professionals
7    LTA
8    Clericals
9    Temp Service/Hourly
10   Other/Misc
11
12   Supplies and Expenses       @SUM(B14..B19)
13   -------------------------------------
14   Supplies
15   Communication
16   Stationery
17   Utilities
18   Contractual Services
19   Other/Misc
20
02-Dec-88  09:54 AM


A21: [W30] 'Equipment                                                    READY


                   A                        B              C         D
21   Equipment                   @SUM(B23..B27)
22   -------------------------------------
23   Furniture
24   Motor vehicle
25   AV
26   Computers/Terminals
27   Other/Misc
28
29   Books & Materials           @SUM(B31..B36)
30   -------------------------------------
31   Books
32   Serials
33   AV/Microforms
34   Binding
35   Services
36   Other/Misc
37
38   Other                       @SUM(B40..B44)
39   -------------------------------------
40   Building and Repair
02-Dec-88  09:55 AM
```

Continued

FIGURE 17-1 *Continued*

```
A60: [W30]                                                          READY


                    A                      B                 C          D
   41   Local Travel
   42   Out of town travel
   43   Contingency
   44   Other/Misc
   45
   46   Total Budget:          +B38+B29+B21+B12+B4
   47
   48
   49
   50
   51
   52   Salaries and Wages     @SUM(B6..B10)
   53   Supplies and Expenses  @SUM(B14..B19)
   54   Equipment              @SUM(B23..B27)
   55   Books & Materials      @SUM(B31..B36)
   56   Other                  @SUM(B40..B44)
   57
   58
   59
   60
   02-Dec-88   09:56 AM
```

absolute (@SUM(b6..b10)). Then use the graph function: /gtp (graph type pie), specify the A and X ranges (the values and the headings), view (if your configuration permits the viewing of graphs), save, and then print, using the PrintGraph disk.

18 TIMESHEETS

PROBLEM
There are a lot of part-time workers in my library, and I need a way of keeping track of exactly how many hours they have worked during the year. Can Lotus help?

COMMANDS
Range format date (/rfd: chapter 2)
Range input (/ri: chapter 2)
Range protect (/rp: chapter 2)
Worksheet column hide (/wch: chapter 1)
Worksheet column-width set (/wcs: chapter 1).

FUNCTIONS
@DATE, @INT, @MOD, and @SUM (chapter 10).

CONCEPTS
Absolute and relative cell addresses (chapter 3).

Though it may seem to be an easy task to keep track of the total amount of time a person works, converting from minutes to hours can be a problem, and mistakes can happen. Lotus eliminates the mistakes; as long as the proper number of hours and minutes worked are entered, Lotus will do the rest.

To keep track of time worked, eight columns will be necessary: the first three are those which will be used by the person entering the information; the next two will show the totals; and the last three will be used by Lotus for computing these totals.

The first column should be formatted for date (/rfd), and the column width should be adjusted to accommodate the date format chosen (/wcs). Remember to use the @DATE function when entering the dates in this column.

The second and third columns are for the hours and minutes worked, respectively. These are entered as whole numbers rather than whole numbers and fractions. Lotus will take these numbers and use them in the last three columns to get the totals for the fourth and fifth columns.

Two of the three remaining columns are used to convert the total minutes into hours and minutes. One column uses the @MOD function; the other uses the @INT function. The @MOD function gives the remainder after a division; the @INT function gives the whole number portion of a division. These are used as follows:

@MOD(@SUM($C$6..C6),60)
@INT(@SUM($C$6..C6)/60)

The first of the functions tells Lotus to obtain the remainder of the sum of the numbers in cells C6 through C6 divided by 60. The dollar signs are used in the first cell location to make the reference absolute: when this formula is copied using the copy command (/c), the first cell address remains the same while the other is automatically adjusted, thus giving a running total. In a similar manner, the @INT function tells Lotus to obtain the integer portion of the division of the sum of the numbers in the cells C6 through C6 divided by 60.

Finally, the sum of the hours worked is obtained, and the number obtained from the @INT function (from the F column in this example) is added to it using an @SUM function:

@SUM($B$6..B6)+G6

This function can also be copied using the copy command (/c), and a running total will be provided. This function is in the column that

84 USING LOTUS 1-2-3

has the total hours. The total minutes column can be either the one with the @MOD function or one that simply copies the information from the @MOD column. (To copy the value from one cell to another, you can use +G7 in the cell which you want the contents of cell G7 to be placed.)

Protect the cells containing the functions: use /rp (range protect) or /ri (range input); in the more recent releases of Lotus, you can use /wch (worksheet column hide).

Figure 18-1

```
FIGURE 18-1

TIMESHEETS
===============
DATE         HOURS      MINUTES    TOTAL      TOTAL
             WORKED     WORKED     HOURS      MINUTES
------------------------------------------------
                                   +H6        +F6        @MOD(@SUM($C$6..C6),60)     @INT(@SUM($C$6..C6)/60)     @SUM($B$6..B6)+G6
                                   +H7        +F7        @MOD(@SUM($C$6..C7),60)     @INT(@SUM($C$6..C7)/60)     @SUM($B$6..B7)+G7
                                   +H8        +F8        @MOD(@SUM($C$6..C8),60)     @INT(@SUM($C$6..C8)/60)     @SUM($B$6..B8)+G8
                                   +H9        +F9        @MOD(@SUM($C$6..C9),60)     @INT(@SUM($C$6..C9)/60)     @SUM($B$6..B9)+G9
                                   +H10       +F10       @MOD(@SUM($C$6..C10),60)    @INT(@SUM($C$6..C10)/60)    @SUM($B$6..B10)+G10
                                   +H11       +F11       @MOD(@SUM($C$6..C11),60)    @INT(@SUM($C$6..C11)/60)    @SUM($B$6..B11)+G11
                                   +H12       +F12       @MOD(@SUM($C$6..C12),60)    @INT(@SUM($C$6..C12)/60)    @SUM($B$6..B12)+G12
                                   +H13       +F13       @MOD(@SUM($C$6..C13),60)    @INT(@SUM($C$6..C13)/60)    @SUM($B$6..B13)+G13
                                   +H14       +F14       @MOD(@SUM($C$6..C14),60)    @INT(@SUM($C$6..C14)/60)    @SUM($B$6..B14)+G14
                                   +H15       +F15       @MOD(@SUM($C$6..C15),60)    @INT(@SUM($C$6..C15)/60)    @SUM($B$6..B15)+G15
                                   +H16       +F16       @MOD(@SUM($C$6..C16),60)    @INT(@SUM($C$6..C16)/60)    @SUM($B$6..B16)+G16
                                   +H17       +F17       @MOD(@SUM($C$6..C17),60)    @INT(@SUM($C$6..C17)/60)    @SUM($B$6..B17)+G17
                                   +H18       +F18       @MOD(@SUM($C$6..C18),60)    @INT(@SUM($C$6..C18)/60)    @SUM($B$6..B18)+G18
                                   +H19       +F19       @MOD(@SUM($C$6..C19),60)    @INT(@SUM($C$6..C19)/60)    @SUM($B$6..B19)+G19
                                   +H20       +F20       @MOD(@SUM($C$6..C20),60)    @INT(@SUM($C$6..C20)/60)    @SUM($B$6..B20)+G20
```

Worksheet printed using Sideways

19 CIRCULATION

PROBLEM
I want to print form letters to tell the patrons when their books are overdue; I have files of their names and addresses on Lotus.

COMMANDS
Copy (/c: chapter 3)
Data query extract (/dqe: chapter 9)
Data sort (/ds: chapter 9)
File save (/fs: chapter 6)
File save replace (/fs~r: chapter 6)
Move (/m: chapter 4)
Print printer (/pp: chapter 7)
Range erase (chapter 2)
Range input (/ri: chapter 2)
Range name create (/rnc: chapter 2)
Range protect (/rp: chapter 2)
Worksheet column hide (/wch: chapter 1)
Worksheet column-width set (/wcs: chapter 1)
Worksheet insert row (/wir: chapter 1).

FUNCTIONS
@NA (chapter 10).

CONCEPTS
End key (introduction) and macros (chapter 13).

Figure 19-1

To create form letters with Lotus, you have to create a worksheet with three parts:
  1. The information that will be inserted into the form letters (in this case, the names and addresses of the patrons)
  2. The form letter itself. (Though Lotus does not have word processing capabilities, a simple form letter can be written into a worksheet; suggestions will follow.)
  3. Macros that will actually do the insertion of the information into the form letters.

The three areas must be completely separate on the worksheet. Make sure the areas do not overlap in terms of columns. This is necessary because the macro will manipulate data in columns, and you must make sure that only the desired information is manipulated.

Whatever release of Lotus you are using, you can set up the worksheet as follows:

Column A: Name. (Put the last name first so that sorting of the names will be possible.) You should adjust the column width (using /wcs: worksheet column-width set) to about 25 characters just to be certain that you will have enough room for the name.

Column B: Street address; adjust the column width (using /wcs: worksheet column-width set).

Column C: City, State, and Zip code; adjust the column width (using /wcs: worksheet column-width set).

Column E: The letter. This column will have the text of the form letter, and so the width should be adjusted (use /wcs: worksheet column-width set) to about 60 or 70. Be sure to leave the patron's name and address areas blank, but note the exact cells into which this information will be inserted. In the example that follows, E11 was reserved for the patron's name, E12 for the patron's street address, and E13 for the patron's city, state, and zip code.

Somewhere outside of columns A through E you will place the macro. In the following example, column G was used to place the macro name (\f) and column H for the macro itself. Placing the name of the macro in the cell adjacent to it helps you to remember how to invoke the particular macro.

Leave the first line of each column of the entire worksheet blank. When the macro is activated, information from below it will be moved into the blank row and inserted into the form letter from that first row. Anything that you have in the first row will be replaced and not printed by this macro. You could place column headings in the first row, as these headings need not be inserted into the form letter.

You may want to sort your information before you print it; in that way, you can print the overdue notices in alphabetical order.

85

```
FIGURE 19-1

A1: [W25] 'Name                                                                              READY


                    A                          B                         C
  1   Name                          Address
  2   Last, First 1                 Address 1                City, State. Zip
  3   Last, First 2                 Address 2                City, State Zip
  4   Last, First 3                 Address 3                City, State Zip
  5   Last, First 4                 Address 4                City, State Zip
  6                                      NA                       NA                      NA
  7
  8
  9
 10
 11
 12
 13
 14
 15
 16
 17
 18
 19
 20
27-Mar-88   04:28 PM
```

In addition, by sorting you will be able to maintain an alphabetical list of patrons with overdue material. To sort, use /ds (data sort), specify the columns A through C as the range, and column A as the primary sort key.

At this point, save the list. If you do not save it, the macro will destroy the data and you will have to input it again. To save the information, use /fs (file save). As you add information to this worksheet, you can update the saved list by replacing the file (/fs˜r: file save replace), using the same name for the new file.

At the end of the list that comprises columns A through C, place @NA in each of the columns; only the NA will appear on the worksheet. This symbol will be read by the macro; when it is read, the macro will stop.

In column E, type the form letter. You can type your library's name, address, and phone number near the top of the page. Skip a few lines (using the arrow keys) for the insertion of the patron information from columns A through C and make note of the exact cells that will be used for this information.

Now, type the text of your letter, making sure that you do not type past the edge of the column. Lotus does not automatically wrap words around as most word processors do; a little care will go a long way here. When it is in finished form, move the cursor to cell G1. (You can use the arrow keys or the GOTO key, the function key F5.) Here type the name by which the macro will be invoked; you will use the same name when you name the macro. In the example, the macro was named \f. Note that the \ is the repeat key, and if you simply type \f, the entire cell will be filled with the letter F when you either depress the enter key or move the cursor to another cell. To avoid this, use a label prefix such as ' before \f.

Move the cursor to H1 and begin typing the macro: each line of the macro is explained:

{GOTO}a2~

The GOTO (enclosed in braces) directs the cursor to move to cell A2.

'/m{END}{DOWN}{END}{RIGHT}~a1~

The ' is a label prefix, which is necessary before each line of the macro that calls for the menu (the / obtains the menu). The m is for the move command that places Lotus in the point mode; the rest of the directions tell Lotus which way to move, highlighting the range to be moved. In this case, the entire list of names and addresses is highlighted. The ~ is the symbol for the enter key. After the range has been entered, A1 tells Lotus where to move the indicated range, which in this case is beginning in cell A1. The ~ is the enter key.

'/ca1~e11~

The ' is the label prefix. The / brings up the menu; c is for copy. You are now copying from cell A1 to the line in the text of the form letter in which the name is to appear. In the example, this is cell E11.

'/cb1~e12~

As in the last line, this copies the information from cell B1 to the line in the text of the form letter in which the street address is to appear. In the example, this is cell E12.

'/cc1~e13~

This copies the contents of cell C1 to cell E13, which is where, in the example, the city, state, and zip code are to appear in the form letter.

```
FIGURE 19-2

G1: '\f                                                          READY


        G        H          I       J        K        L        M        N
  1   \f       {GOTO}a2~
  2            /m{END}{DOWN}{END}{RIGHT}~a1~
  3            /ca1~e11~
  4            /cb1~e12~
  5            /cc1~e13~
  6            /xi@isna(a1)~/xq
  7            /ppre1..e28~gpq
  8            /xg\f~
  9
 10
 11
 12
 13
 14
 15
 16
 17
 18
 19
 20
27-Mar-88   06:03 PM
```

'/xi@isna(a1)~/xq
The label prefix begins the line, as it does in many lines of a macro. Following the label prefix is the equivalent of an if statement: if NA appears in cell A1, do what follows on this line, which is to quit running the macro (/xq). Remember that you typed @NA at the end of each of the columns and when the NA appears in cell A1, the entire list has been processed and the macro will stop. If NA does not appear in cell A1, the if statement tells the macro to continue to the next line for more instructions.

'/ppre1..e28~gpq
If NA does not appear in cell A1, the macro instructs Lotus to get the menu (/), choose print (p), select printer, and then select the range, which is the form letter. In the example, the form letter occupies cells E1 through E28. The length of the form letter is not important, as long as your letter does not exceed one page. Then Lotus is told to go ahead and print (g), advance the paper to the top of the page in the printer (p), and quit the print menu (q).

Figure 19-2

'/xg\f˜
This line actually tells Lotus to go back to the beginning of the macro in order to continue processing the items in columns A through C. The macro does this by using a /xg command, which instructs Lotus to continue the macro by going to \f, which is what this entire macro was named. Thus a loop is formed, and the operation will continue until @NA is encountered in cell A1: at that point, the macro will cease operating.

A modification that can be made is to include a column for date due (format for date using range format date, /rfd; adjust column-width using worksheet column-width set, /wcs) and then sort or extract only those which meet certain criteria. If you use this modification, be sure to adjust the macro column specifications to account for the extra column. In addition, if you will be using data query extract (/dqe) to extract by date due, be sure to specify your criterion and output ranges completely separate from the other areas of the worksheet. You may want to save the worksheet with these ranges specified.

If you are using one of the more recent releases of Lotus, you can modify the macro slightly: the macro (as written above) places the patron's name into the letter as last name, first name. The newer releases allow you to get the order of the names correct; instead of three columns of information of patron information, four are used: A: last name; B: first name; C: street address; D: city, state, and zip. Be sure to type @NA at the end of each of the columns. The new macro is as follows:

{GOTO}a2˜
Moves cursor to cell A2.

'/m{END}{DOWN}{END}{RIGHT}˜a1˜
The move command and highlighting of the range to be moved and the left hand corner of the range to be moved to.

{LET f11,+b1&" "&+a1}
Place the information from cell B1 (in the example the patron's first name) followed by a blank space (" ") followed by the information from cell A1 (in the example, the patron's last name) in cell F11 (which in the example is where the patron's name is to be placed in the form letter: note that all the columns were shifted in order to accommodate the additional column needed for the patron information). The & symbol is used to connect the pieces of information that are to appear in the indicated cell.

{LET f12, + c1}

This places the information that appeared in cell C1 (the street address of the patron) into cell F12.

{LET f13, + d1}

This places the information that appeared in cell D1 (the city, state, and zip code of the patron) into cell F13.

{LET f15, + "Dear "& + b1&" "&a1&","}

In a refinement of the original macro, this line permits the first line of the form letter to be Dear (first name) (last name). Lotus does this by letting cell f15 (which is two lines below the city, state, and zip code of the patron) to be filled by the word Dear, followed by a blank space, followed by the contents of cell B1 (patron's first name), then the contents of cell A1 (patron's last name), followed by a comma (","). As in the third line of this modified macro, the parts of the LET statement are connected by &, and the entire statement is enclosed in braces.

'/xi@isna(a1)~/xq

If the contents of cell A1 is @NA, stop the execution of the macro. If A! contains anything other than @NA, continue to the next line of the macro for further instructions.

'/pprf1..f28~gpq

If cell A1 does not contain @NA, continue by printing the entire form letter: the range is specified as F1..F28; after the letter has been printed (g), the printer advances to the top of the page (p) and the print menu is quit (q).

'/xg\f~

Continue the macro (which you named \f) by returning to its beginning.

When you have finished writing the macro, you must name it using the range name create command (/rnc). Place the cursor on the first cell of macro, then name it (in the example, \f has been used). If the cursor had been placed in the first cell of the macro, depressing the enter key for the range is all that is necessary: only the first cell of the macro needs to be specified. The macro will continue operating until it is instructed to quit or until it reaches a blank cell.

At this point, you should have the patron information, the form letter, and the macro: protect the cells that contain the macro (as well as the form letter if desired). To protect, you can use one of

Figure 19-3

```
FIGURE 19-3

J1:  '\x                                                                    READY


         J          K           L         M         N         O         P         Q
 1    \x         {GOTO}a2~
 2               /m{END}{DOWN}{END}{RIGHT}~a1~
 3               {let f11,+b1&" "&+a1}
 4               {let f12,+c1}
 5               {let f13,+d1}
 6               /xi@isna(a1)~/xq
 7               /pprf1..f28~gpq
 8               /xg\x~
 9
10
11
12
13
14
15
16
17
18
19
20
27-Mar-88   05:48 PM
```

several methods: either use /rp (range protect), /ri (range input), or even /wch (worksheet column hide: available only on the later releases of Lotus). Then save the entire worksheet (/fs: file save). Then run the macro: you may want to try it with a small trial list of patrons to test it and see how the form letter looks.

The following is another macro that might aid you in having the patron information updated; this macro will prompt the person entering the data for the proper input:

{GOTO}a2~{END}{DOWN}{DOWN}

This line moves the cursor to the beginning of the list and then finds the first available row to enter data into. Before beginning to enter data, you should delete the @NA from the last row or simply use the macro without the final {DOWN} on this line: the cursor will stop at the line marked @NA. Another way around this is to insert lines between the last line used and the @NA line. To insert lines, you would use /wir (worksheet insert rows).

'/xlName: ~~

This line uses an /xl command, which displays the textual information that follows. In this case, the textual information is the prompt for patron's name. If you are using the macro designed for the later releases of Lotus, your prompt macro line will probably be '/xlLast Name: ~~. Instead of /xl, {GETLABEL} can be used with the later releases of Lotus.

{RIGHT}

This command moves the cursor one cell to the right.

'/xlStreet: ~~

This line uses the /xl command to indicate a prompt for the street. If you are using the macro designed for the later releases of Lotus, you will insert another two macro lines to prompt for the First Name and then to move the cursor right one cell. To do this, you would use:

'/xlFirst Name: ~~
{RIGHT}

{RIGHT}

This moves the cursor one cell to the right.

'/xlCity, State, Zip: ""

This line prompts the person entering data to enter the city, state, and zip code of the patron.

'/xg\e~

This line returns the macro to the beginning of this macro, which has been named \e. By returning to the beginning, the cursor is moved to cell A2, down to the end of the column, and then down one more cell, which is the next empty cell in the first column.

At this point, the macro must be named, using the /rnc (range name create) command. In the example, the macro was named \e; if you have your cursor on the first line of this macro, you can specify the range by simply depressing the enter key: only the first line of a macro needs to be entered for its range.

The only way to get out of this loop is to simultaneously depress the control and break keys. This is a good time for a supervisor to intervene; it is also a good time for the file to be saved (/fs: file save; if this is an updating of an existing file, you can use /fs~r: file save replace).

The above macro can be modified to give the person inputting

Figure 19-4

FIGURE 19-4

```
S1: '{GOTO}a2~{END}{DOWN}{DOWN}                                    READY

              O         P         Q         R         S         T         U         V
    1                                       \e        {GOTO}a2~{END}{DOWN}{DOWN}
    2                                                 /xlName: ~~
    3                                                 {RIGHT}
    4                                                 /xlStreet: ~~
    5                                                 {RIGHT}
    6                                                 /xlCity,State,Zip: ~~
    7                                                 /xg\e~
    8
    9
   10
   11
   12
   13
   14
   15
   16
   17
   18
   19
   20
27-Mar-88  06:09 PM
```

information a chance to break out of the loop. This process is accomplished through the use of a /xm or, in the more recent releases of Lotus, {MENUBRANCH} command, which actually halts the macro and permits the user a choice; in this case, it is a choice between continuing on to another entry and quitting. The quitting option automatically sorts the file by patron name and then saves the file, replacing the original file with the updated one. This is accomplished as follows:

{GOTO}A2˜{END}{DOWN}{DOWN}
'/xlName: ˜˜
{RIGHT}
'/xlStreet: ˜˜
{RIGHT}
'/xlCity, State, Zip: ˜˜

These lines are exactly as they were in the original macro. If your worksheet contains separate columns for first and last names, two additional lines will have to be inserted before the /xl command request for the street address:

'/xlFirst name: ~
{RIGHT}

'/xmz1~
At this point, the macro continues with a user-defined menu which has Z1 as its upper left hand cell. Z1 was chosen to be out of the way of all other worksheet functions and entries. At this point, the macro divides in two parts, one for each of the menu options. The two options are presented in cells Z1 and AA1; brief explanations of these options appear in cells Z2 and AA2. The menu choices can be made as all menu choices in Lotus: either by moving the highlighter using the arrow keys and then depressing the enter key or by depressing the first letter of the choice. Each strand of the macro will be discussed separately.

(Beginning at Z1): More
A label prefix is not required because this is a textual line in a macro. This choice would be made if the user had more information to input. When the cellpointer is on this option, the brief explanation which was typed in cell Z2 appears: Add more names.

(Continuing the More option): {DOWN}{END}{LEFT}
'/xg\m~
These two lines are similar to those in the macro explained above. This macro was named \m, using the /rnc (range name create) command.

(Beginning at AA1): Quit
A label prefix is not required because this is a textual line in a macro. If the user has no more information to input, the quit option is chosen. When the cellpointer is on the word quit, the brief description typed in cell AA2 is displayed: No more to add.

(Continuing the quit option): {GOTO}a2~
The cursor is moved to the beginning of the file. Remember, the first line of the patron information database has been left empty so that the form letter macro will work correctly.

(Continuing the quit option):'/dsrd.{END}{DOWN}{END}{RIGHT}~
This line gets the menu (/), selects data sort (ds), resets the settings (r), and defines the range (d), which is specified by entering the point mode (.), anchoring the range at cell A2, and highlighting the entire database.

(Continuing the quit option): pa2~a~
The primary sort key is defined as the first column (name or last name), and ascending order has been specified.

(Continuing the quit option): sb2~a~
The secondary sort key is defined as the second column (first name), and ascending order has been specified. This line is only necessary if separate columns were used for the patrons' first and last names.

(Continuing the quit option): g~q
Go ahead and sort, and then quit the data menu.

(Continuing the quit option): '/fs~r
Replace the existing file with the updated one, using the same name.

One further macro that may save time for the person using form letters in the circulation department of a library: when a patron clears his or her account, the name, etc. should be removed from

Figure 19-5
Figure 19-6

FIGURE 19-5

```
R1: '\m                                                              READY


         R         S         T         U         V         W         X         Y
  1      \m        {GOTO}a2~{END}{DOWN}{DOWN}
  2                /xlName: ~~
  3                {RIGHT}
  4                /xlStreet: ~~
  5                {RIGHT}
  6                /xlCity,State,Zip: ~~
  7                /xmz1~
  8
  9
 10
 11
 12
 13
 14
 15
 16
 17
 18
 19
 20
30-Nov-88    10:26 AM
```

```
FIGURE 19-6

AA8:   '/fs~r                                                              READY


                Z         AA        AB        AC        AD        AE        AF        AG
 1     More      Quit
 2     Add more  No more
 3     /xg\m~    {GOTO}a2~
 4               /dsrd.{END}{DOWN}{END}{RIGHT}~
 5               pa2~a~
 6               sb2~a~
 7               g~q
 8               /fs~r
 9
10
11
12
13
14
15
16
17
18
19
20
30-Nov-88  10:27 AM
```

the list; otherwise, the patron will continue to receive letters. Removing names from the list can be accomplished in several ways.

One way is to find the name on the list, use /re (range erase), specify the range, which would be from column A through either column C (if you are using an older release of Lotus) or column D (if you are using a more recent release of Lotus). Then, you have to close the gap in the worksheet because the macros that have been written only work on continuous worksheets (i.e., no blank cells). To close up the gaps, you can use the /m (move) command, specifying the from and to move ranges. There is an easier way: a macro.

'/re
Range erase

{END}{RIGHT}~
This line defines the range to be deleted: the entire line related to the person whose record has been cleared. The ~ is the symbol for the enter key.

{DOWN}
The cellpointer is moved down one line; the A column of the next entry is highlighted.

'/m.{END}{DOWN}{END}{RIGHT}~
The area to be moved is highlighted by anchoring the range to the first cell (which is the A column of the line below that which has been erased) and highlighting the entire worksheet after that point. The return completes the range to be moved.

{UP}~
In response to the question of where the highlighted information is to be moved, only the upper left hand cell needs to be indicated; in this case, the indicated cell is one line above the indicated range. The enter symbol (~) completes the operation.

It should be noted that for this macro to work properly, the cellpointer must be placed in the left-most cell of the information about the person who has cleared his or her record. Be sure to name the macro using /rnc (range name create).

Figure 19-7

```
FIGURE 19-7

AD6:                                                              READY

           AD       AE       AF       AG       AH       AI       AJ       AK
   1   /re
   2   {END}{RIGHT}~
   3   {DOWN}
   4   /m.{END}{DOWN}{END}{RIGHT}~
   5   {UP}~
   6
   7
   8
   9
  10
  11
  12
  13
  14
  15
  16
  17
  18
  19
  20
  27-Mar-88   04:48 PM
```

20 OVERDUES

PROBLEM
How can I easily compute fines for overdue books?

COMMANDS
Copy (/c: chapter 3)
Range format currency (/rfc: chapter 2)
Range format date (/rfd: chapter 2)
Range input (/ri: chapter 2)
Range name create (/rnc: chapter 2)
Range protect (/rp: chapter 2)
Worksheet column hide (/wch: chapter 1)
Worksheet column-width set (/wcs: chapter 1)
Worksheet global column-width set (/wgcs: chapter 1)

FORMULAS AND FUNCTIONS
Addition, division, multiplication, and subtraction (chapter 10), @DATE, @IF, @INT, and @TODAY (chapter 10).

CONCEPTS
Absolute cell addresses (chapter 3) and macros (chapter 13).

Computing overdue fines is an easy process using Lotus's date functions, because Lotus is able to compute the number of days between two given dates; multiplying the remainder by the overdue fine is simple.

Using the cells from A1 through B4 is all that it takes. Cell A1 is used for the title of the worksheet (in the example Library Fines has been used). Adjust column width to 15 (/wgcs15: worksheet global column-width set). Because this width is needed for all the columns used on this worksheet, the worksheet global column-width command is used instead of worksheet column-width set (/wcs). Furthermore, the title was underlined using the repeat key and the = sign (\=). When the enter key is depressed after combination is entered, the = sign is repeated across the entire cell, double underlining the title.

Cell A3 is used for the heading Date Due. Cell A4 is used for the heading Returned Date. Cell A6 is used for the heading Amount Due. Only column B, cells 3 and 4, are formatted for date (/rfd: range format date). To enter a date in one of these cells, you must use the following function:

@DATE(year,month,day)

In the function statement, the year is a two-digit year, the month and day can be either one or two digits as necessary. Lotus transforms the date that you enter into the date format that you have selected by changing the date into a number (the count is from the first day of the year in 1900) and then changing that number into a date. The intervening number (which is not seen) can then be used for date calculations, such as determining the amount of time between two dates.

In cell B4, you can either enter the date returned using the @DATE function in the same manner, or, if the date is the current day, you can use the following function (if you entered the date in response to the DOS prompt when you began operating your computer for the day):

@TODAY

This function inserts the present date into the highlighted cell that is formatted for date.

Cell B6 should be formatted for currency with two decimal

98

places (/rfc2: range format currency with two decimal places). Then, use the following formula to compute the amount due:

(+B4-B3)*.05

This formula assumes that the fine is five cents per day overdue; other fine amounts can be substituted for .05.

If your library does not charge overdue fines for the days on which it is closed (such as Sundays), it is possible to build this into the worksheet. To accomplish this, you will have to write a short macro to let the user choose the day of the week on which the transaction is taking place. To accomplish this, you will have to use a {MENUBRANCH} command (/xm for those using an earlier release of Lotus):

{MENUBRANCH cell location}

The cell location tells Lotus where to look for the left-most menu choice on the menu you are creating. In this case, the days of the week, Monday through Saturday, are listed. Each of the six days of the week leads Lotus on its own path; though the paths are similar, each one is slightly different.

As an example, we will follow the path of the {MENUBRANCH} choice Monday; as the logic is explained, the other days will logically follow. In column H (for example), the following will be found:

Cell	Contents
H1	{MENUBRANCH h2}
H2	Monday
H3	Today

Meaning: the cell under the menu choice tells what the choice means. In this case, the word indicates that if today is Monday, choose this option.

H4   '/ch7~b6~

Meaning: Copy the cell H7 to cell B6. On this worksheet, cell h7 computes the amount of money that is owed to the library, and B6 is where the amount due is recorded.

H6   (b4-b3)-@INT(b4-b3)/7)

Meaning: this complicated-looking formula instructs Lotus to:
1. Subtract the serial number of the date in cell B3 (date due) from the serial number of the date in cell B4 (date returned). This produces the number of days that the book is overdue.
2. Perform the same subtraction as above (serial number of date returned minus the serial number of date due), divide the number by seven, the number of days in the week. Using the function @INT produces only the integer portion of the dividend: this is the number of Sundays that occurred in the period between the date due and the date returned.
3. The remainder in step 2 (above) is subtracted from the remainder in step 1 (above).

H7   @IF($H$6>0#and#$H$6<7,
       ($H$6-1)*.05,$H$6*.05)

Meaning: This complicated looking @IF function tells Lotus to examine the value produced by the formula in H6 above, and then:
1. If the value in H6 is more than 0 and less than 7 (the first part of the @IF statement which presents the condition to be tested), subtract 1 from that value (in H6). This step is necessary because in the formula in cell H6, Sundays could not be counted if the book is less than seven days overdue. As Mondays are one day after Sundays, the first part of the @IF statement details that if the number produced in H6 is more than 0 and less than 7, subtract one. This line will vary for other days of the week as follows: for Tuesdays, it will be more than 1 and less than 7; for Wednesdays, more than 2 and less than 7; for Thursdays, more than 3 and less than 7; Fridays, more than 4 and less than 7; Saturdays, more than 5 and less than 7. Then, multiply this number by .05 (the fine per day).
2. If the condition in the first part of the @IF statmement is not true, then simply use the value in H6 and multiply it by the fine per day, in this case .05.

The number produced in this cell is then copied into cell B6 using the copy command (/c). In the formula in cell H6 you may have noticed that the addresses of all the cells are absolute (note the dollar signs on both the column and row designations). If these are not absolute addresses, the cell addresses will be adjusted when the

OVERDUES **101**

Figure 20-1

cell is copied to cell B6, causing the amount due to be totally incorrect.

The macro can be adjusted if the library is closed for more than one day during the week (perhaps during the summer or vacation times).

Similar branches are created for each of the days of the week: if you want to copy the information in cell H6 to the other days of the week, be sure the cell addresses are absolute (i.e. $B$4). Since the addresses in cell H7 are already absolute, the cell can be copied easily (use the copy command, /c).

The entire macro should be placed in a portion of the worksheet that cannot be seen by the user: it is rather distracting with all the functions and values. In addition, the portion of the worksheet that contains the macro should be protected in some way (you can use either /rp, range protect or /ri, range input; in the more recent releases of Lotus, you can simply hide the columns using /wch, worksheet column hide).

The macro has to be named, using the /rnc (range name create) command. Before beginning the command, place the cursor on the first line of the macro: in this way, after you have named the macro (\a in this example), you can simply depress the enter key to indicate the range because only the first cell in the macro needs to be indicated. The portion of the worksheet that will remain visible and unprotected will look like this:

LIBRARY FINES

(A3) Due Date:
(A4) Returned Date:
(A5) Depress Alt and A
(A6) Amount Due

FIGURE 20-1

```
LIBRARY FINES                  {MENUBRANCH d2}
================               Mon         Tues        Wed         (Thurs)     Fri         Sat
Due Date:        04-Jul-87     Today       Today       Today       Today       Today       Today
Returned Date:   07-Jul-87     /cd7~b6~    /ce7~b6~    /cf7~b6~    /cg7~b6~    /ch7~b6~    /ci7~b6~
Depress Alt and a
Amount Due:         $0.10              3           3           3           3           3           3
                                    $0.10       $0.10       $0.10       $0.15       $0.15       $0.15
```

Worksheet printed using Sideways

Cell A5 gives the user instructions: depress the Alt key and A: this invokes the macro (described above) which computes the fine, which will be copied to cell B6. In the example, the macro has been named \a.

21 PERIODICALS

PROBLEM
Can Lotus help me create a list of the periodicals held in my library?

COMMANDS
Copy (/c: chapter 3)
Data fill (/df chapter 9)
Data query extract (/dqe: chapter 9)
Data query find (/dqf: chapter 9)
Data sort (/ds: chapter 9)
File save (/fs: chapter 6)
Range erase (/re: chapter 2)
Range name create (/rnc: chapter 2)
Worksheet column hide (/wch: chapter 1)
Worksheet column-width set (/wcs: chapter 1)
Worksheet global column-width set (/wgcs: chapter 1)
Worksheet global protect (/wgp: chapter 1)
Worksheet global unprotect (/wgu: chapter 1)
Worksheet titles horizontal (/wth: chapter 1)

FUNCTIONS
@DAVG, @DCOUNT, @DMAX, @DMIN, and @DSUM (chapter 10)

CONCEPTS
End key (introduction) and macros (chapter 13).

Creating a database with Lotus will enable you to produce a list of the periodicals held in your library. Instead of numbers, in this case your worksheet will be filled with text, which Lotus will manipulate.

To begin, widen the columns for the entire worksheet to 20 (/wgcs20: worksheet global column-width set 20) to accommodate long text. If any column needs more or less room, use /wcs (worksheet column-width set) to adjust an individual column.

The title of the journal will be entered in column A. Column B will contain the library's holdings. Column C will contain information on how the item is held (paper copy, microfilm). Columns D and E will contain subjects (more than two columns can be used for subjects). The subject headings can be obtained from many different sources, or can be created to suit the needs of the individual library. Column F will contain the language in which the journal is published. A final column can be added to keep track of the cost of each subscription. If this column is added, you may wish to conceal the information from the users if this list is going to be available on a microcomputer (use /wch: worksheet column hide if a recent release of Lotus is being used). If the list is to be printed, simply do not specify this column as part of the range for printing.

After the column headings have been entered along the top row, place the cursor in cell A2 and use /wth (worksheet titles horizontal) to keep the column headings on screen at all times. This will aid in the compilation of the list by keeping the person entering data from confusing the columns. In addition, if you are going to have the list available on a microcomputer, having the column headings on screen will aid the users.

If the list is to be available on a microcomputer, you will probably want to protect the entire worksheet; this will prohibit users from making changes on the list. To protect the worksheet, use /wgp (worksheet global protect).

Once the data is in the file, several manipulations will be possible. Before performing any of them, save the worksheet (/fs: file save) and take the protection off (/wgu: worksheet global unprotect). After that, modifying existing information is easy. You can change the contents of a cell in the identical way that you would change information in any cell of a worksheet. Simply position the cursor on the cell and, to replace the entire contents simply write over it. To edit the contents of the cell, depress the function key F2 (edit) and make the necessary changes. To erase the contents of a cell, use /re (range erase).

If you need to add entries (a new title has been added), simply add it to the end of the list. Then use the data sort command (/ds) to arrange the entire list in alphabetical order. Define the range as the entire worksheet (minus the column headings), select the title as the primary sort, and the order as ascending. Then, let Lotus sort the list.

You can also use data sort (/ds) to create lists of periodicals by subject. As in the data sort described above, the range will be the entire worksheet excluding the line with the column headings, but the primary sort will be the column with the subject headings if only one column were used for subject headings. Once again, ascending order is chosen. The secondary sort key is used in this case: the title column should be chosen, once again in ascending order. Then let Lotus go ahead and sort: a list of journals in alphabetical order by subject will be produced.

If you need a list of journals in one subject area, you can use the data query extract (/dqe) command. This command can be used to obtain a subject list even if more than one column was used for subject headings. Set up the input range, criterion range, and output range: the input range is what Lotus is to select from (the entire worksheet would be appropriate, including the column headings, which must be included); the criterion range sets up the record selection criteria, with the first line being the column headings and subsequent line(s) listing the criteria for selection; the output range is a blank portion of the worksheet onto which Lotus will copy the extracted records. These three ranges must be specified before the data query extract (/dqe) can be performed. In this case, you would specify the specific subject headings as the criterion to be searched; use all appropriate column headings in the criterion and output ranges.

If you want to examine the record of one journal, you could use the arrow keys to get to it. This process is slow if you have a long list. Instead, you could use the data query find command (/dqf). This will highlight the record you are seeking. To use data query find, you must first set up the input and criterion ranges; no output range is needed for /dqf (date query find).

If patrons are using the file on the microcomputer, you may want to write macros to help them find the entry they are looking for. To provide several choices for the patron, use the '/xm command to create a menu; in the later releases of Lotus, the {MENUBRANCH} command may be used. Utilizing an unused portion of the worksheet, use the /xm command as follows:

'/xmaa2

This command tells Lotus to find a user-defined menu whose leftmost cell is cell AA2. Four menu choices are then given, in cells

Figure 21-1

AA2, AB2, AC2, and AD2; each of these choices will be discussed separately.

The first menu choice is given in cell AA2: Look. Cell AA3 defines the option: Use arrow keys. In other words, this option permits the user to go through the list manually, one record at a time. This option ends with cell AA4, which simply directs Lotus to move the cursor to the home position: {HOME}.

The second menu option is given in cell AB2: Find. Cell AB3 defines this option: Specific title. In other words, this option permits the user to ascertain whether or not your library's collection contains a specific title. The user must enter the title to be searched for in respose to a Lotus prompt which is given by use of a /xl command:

'/xlTitle to find:˜l2˜

The /xl command posts a message and waits for a response, which it places in the indicated cell, in this case cell L2. In the later releases of Lotus, you can use {GETLABEL} for '/xl.

```
FIGURE 21-1

AB1:                                                              READY


                    Z                  AA                 AB
  1      \a                     /xmAa2~
  2                             Look
  3                             Use arrow keys
  4                             {Home}~
  5
  6
  7
  8
  9
 10
 11
 12
 13
 14
 15
 16
 17
 18
 19
 20
28-Mar-88    09:22 AM
```

Cell L2 is part of the criterion range, which must be specified for a data query find. The entire criterion range contains the column headings, which may be copied from the column headings of the list into the first row of the criterion range using the copy command (/c). The criterion range also contains the definition of what Lotus is to search for, which is in its second row. In this case, the user's response to the /xl command provides the definition of what Lotus is to find. The response is automatically written in the criterion range, in this example, cell L2.

The next line of the macro, to which Lotus will proceed once the /xl command has been finished, is:

'/dqr

The ' is a label prefix, which preceeds all non-textual lines in the macro. It is followed by the /, which obtains the command menu. The d selects data, q selects query, and the r resets the ranges.

The next line is:

i{HOME}.{END}{DOWN}{END}{RIGHT}˜

This line defines the input range. First the cursor is sent to the home position, the . anchors it, and the remainder of the line highlights the entire list, including all the columns and rows.

The next line defines the criterion range, which tells Lotus what to look for:

cl1..l2˜

Since only the title is being searched for, only this much has to be defined as the criterion range. Cell L1 contains the column heading; cell L2 contains the title to be searched, as defined by the user in response to the '/xl message (above).

The last lines are:

f˜{?}{ESC}q
{HOME}

This line tells Lotus to find the indicated title; if it is found, it will be highlighted on the periodicals list. Lotus then pauses for the user to depress a key {?}; then Lotus escapes from the data query menu. The cursor is then sent to the Home position.

The third option on the user defined menu is in cell AC2: Subject. Cell AC3 defines this selection: Subject list. Once again, a

Figure 21-2

```
FIGURE 21-2

AA1:                                                                    READY

                AA              AB                  AC
1
2                        Find
3                        Specific title
4                        /xlTitle to find:~12~
5                        /dqr
6                        i{HOME}.{END}{DOWN}{end}{RIGHT}~
7                        c11..12~
8                        f~~{?}{ESC}q
9                        {HOME}
10
11
12
13
14
15
16
17
18
19
20
30-Nov-88   10:27 AM
```

/xl command is used to permit the user to define the subject for which Lotus is to look:

'/xlSubject to find~P2~

Lotus will display the message Subject to find, and pause for user input, which will be placed in cell P2. Cell P2 is part of the criterion range, which must be defined for the data query extract command, which will be executed. This criterion range is set up exactly as in the previous menu option.

The next two lines are the same as in the previously discussed user defined menu option:

'/dqr
{HOME}.{END}{DOWN}{END}{RIGHT}~

Once again, the data query option is selected, the ranges are reset, and the input range is defined as the entire periodicals list.

The next line defines the output range: an output range is needed for the data query extract (/dqe) command. The output range is where Lotus will copy all the records that match the defined criterion. An unused portion of the worksheet must be used for this; in the example, cells L30 through Q30 contain the column headings, which may be copied from the list using the copy command (/c).

    ol30..q300˜

Thus, the output range is defined as cells l30 through q300.
The criterion range is next defined in the macro:

    cp1..p2˜

This contains the user's response to the /xl message that asked for the subject to be searched.
The next line of this option instructs Lotus to proceed with the extraction of records:

    eq

After extracting, Lotus is told to quit the data query option.
The final line of the macro moves the cursor to the top of the output range so that the user can examine the list that was extracted: {GOTO}l30˜

The final option in the user defined menu is located in cell AD2: Non-English. Cell AD3 defines this option: Language. This option permits the user to locate materials in languages other than English. Though any language can be specified, including English, only non-English languages should be searched, since English will probably constitute the majority of the collection.

The macro proceeds with a /xl message:

    '/xlLanguage to find:˜o2˜

The macro pauses for user input, in this case the language to be searched for, and places the response in cell O2, which is part of the criterion range.
The next two lines are identical to those in the previous menu choices:

Figure 21-3

```
FIGURE 21-3

AD1:                                                                    READY

                AB                  AC                  AD
 1
 2                          Subject
 3                          Subject List
 4                          /xlSubject to find:~p2~
 5                          /dqr
 6                          i{HOME}.{END}{DOWN}{end}{RIGHT}~
 7                          ol30..q300~
 8                          cp1..p2~
 9                          Eq
10                          {GOTO}130~
11
12
13
14
15
16
17
18
19
20
30-Nov-88  10:28 AM
```

'/dqr
i{HOME}.{END}{DOWN}{END}{RIGHT}~

The data query settings are reset, and the input range is defined as the entire periodicals list.

The output range is next defined:

ol30..q300

This output range is identical to the previous output range: it is used to tell Lotus where to place the extracted records.

The next line defines the criterion range:

co1..o2~

Thus, the criterion to be searched for is the language which was specified in response to the /xl prompt.

The final two lines of this menu option's macro are identical to the previous option:

eq
{GOTO}l30~

The macro is completed by telling Lotus to go ahead and extract the records which match the criterion specified, quit the data query menu, and then move the cursor to cell L30, which is the beginning of the output range. The extracted records are here.

The entire macro that begins with the /xm command must be named. Place the cursor on the first cell of the macro (in the example, it is cell AA1), use /rnc (range name create), and name the macro (\a was used in the example).

To prevent users from changing any of the entries, you should protect the entire worksheet: /wgp (worksheet global protect). Then save the entire worksheet (/fs: file save). If you want this file to be automatically retrieved whenever this disk is loaded in conjunction with Lotus, name the file AUTO123.

To alert users to the availability of the macro, a sign should be posted either on or next to the computer, advising them to depress the ALT key and A simultaneously. This will invoke the macro that

Figure 21-4

```
FIGURE 21-4

AC1:                                                                      READY


               AC                    AD                    AE
1
2                          Non-English
3                          Language
4                          /xlLanguage to find:~o2~
5                          /dqr
6                          i{HOME}.{END}{DOWN}{end}{RIGHT}~
7                          o130..q300~
8                          co1..o2~
9                          Eq
10                         {GOTO}l30~
11
12
13
14
15
16
17
18
19
20
29-Mar-88   11:51 AM
```

has the user-defined menu. On the other hand, you could name this macro \0, which will cause the macro to be invoked whenever the worksheet is retrieved.

If the final column, cost, was added, several manipulations can be made using database statistical functions. These functions can, among other things, produce a total (@DSUM), give an average (@DAVG), find the maximum and minumum values (@DMAX and @DMIN), and perform a count (@DCOUNT) on specified segments of a database such as the periodicals list. It is possible to do without these database statistical functions by using several steps, but these functions are powerful and useful.

For example, to find the average cost of subscriptions to business journals in your library, you could extract the business journals using the data query extract command (/dqe), obtain a total cost by using an @SUM function, and then divide by the number of extracted journals, which can be obtained by using the @COUNT function or data fill (/df) command, which will number the items in your list, starting from one and continuing to the end of the list. On the other hand, you could use a database statistical function: @DAVG, which will perform the entire task in one step.

To use a database statistical function, you must provide three ranges of information. First, the database, which is usually the entire database range (specified as a1..g200, for example). Second, the offset, which is the number of the column of the database that contains the values to be used in the database statistical function: the columns start with the number zero for the left-most column and continue to the right in steps of one. Third, the criterion, which defines which entries are to be searched. The criterion must contain two rows, the first of which contains the column headings, which can be copied (using /c) from the column headings of the worksheet, and the second defining which entries are to be selected from the column indicated. The criterion is specified as a range, such as l1..l2.

In the example, the database statistical function could look like this:

@DAVG(a1..g200,6,l1..l2)

This assumes that the database occupies cells A1 through G200, that the column in which the costs per journal are kept is in column G (since the cost is in the seventh column from the left, and the numbering begins with the number zero, this column is referred to in the offset as 6), and that the criterion were specified in cells l1 and l2.

A maximum or minumum cost for the journals in any subject field could be found in a similar manner, using @DMAX and @DMIN. A count could even be performed on the number of journals kept on microfilm or hard copy (@DCOUNT). The cost of subscriptions in Spanish could be obtained using @DSUM. The possibilities of the database statistical functions are endless.

22 REFERENCE

PROBLEM
I need an easy way to keep track of monthly and total year reference statistics. Can Lotus help?

COMMANDS
Copy (/c: chapter 3)
Graph type pie chart (/gtp: chapter 8)
Range format percentage (/rfp: chapter 2)
Worksheet insert row (/wir: chapter 1)

FORMULAS AND FUNCTIONS
Addition and division (chapter 10), @IF, @ISERR, @NA, @SUM (chapter 10)

CONCEPTS
Absolute, mixed and relative cell addresses (chapter 3).

Setting up a worksheet that will keep track of monthly and annual reference statistics relies on the @SUM function. This function will add together the different types of reference questions, providing total volume per month. It will then be used to add together the monthly statistics to provide a year to date total.

Cell A1 should contain the title of the worksheet: REFERENCE STATISTICS, 1987. You can underline the title by placing the cursor in cell A2, depressing the \ and then the -. The \ is the repeat key in Lotus, and the entire cell will be underlined when the enter key is depressed. You can continue the underlining by repeating the operation in cell B2 or by using the copy command (/c).

Column A, from rows 4 through 15, will be used to record the months of the year. Row 3 will be used from column B on to record the types of reference questions. In the sample worksheet, five types of reference questions are differentiated: directional (column B), circulation (column C), periodicals (column D), microforms (column E), and reference (column F).

The last column (column G), as well as the last row (row 16), will be used for totals. In cell G4 the function

@SUM(b4..f4)

is recorded; this function is then copied using the copy command (/c) through cell g15. Lotus automatically adjusts the relative cell addresses. For example, cell G14 will contain the function @SUM(b14..g14).

In a similar manner, cell B16 contains the function:

@SUM(b4..b15)

This function will provide a year-to-date total for the column. This function is then copied across the worksheet using the copy command (/c) to cell F16. Once again, Lotus automatically adjusts the relative cell addresses, providing a year-to-date total for each of the columns of the worksheet. For example, cell E16 will contain the function @SUM(e4..e15).

A total for the entire worksheet can be provided in cell G16:

@SUM(b16..f16)

Or, the same cell could contain the function:

@SUM(g4..g15)

Either way, the total for all catagories for the year to date will be provided in this cell.

Figure 22-1

GRAPHING

You can graph the results of this worksheet. A pie chart would be an effective way to compare the number of questions of each type. To create a pie chart, call up the menu, then choose graph type pie (/gtp). The A range will be the numbers that you want to compare. (If you are dealing with the year to date figures, B16..F16; the X range will be the headings B3 to F3.)

ADDING PERCENTAGES

You may add columns to the worksheet for percentages. In this case, the worksheet will contain twice as many columns. Columns B and C will be used for directional questions, with the number of directional questions placed in column B and the percentage of total questions for the month placed in column C. The remainder of the worksheet will be divided in a similar manner.

You will probably want to insert two more rows after row 3 (use /wir: worksheet insert row). One of these rows will be used to record the column subheadings (number and percent); the other will be used for a solid line (produced with \-, which, when the return key is depressed, will fill the cell with underlining). This cell is then copied across the worksheet using the copy command (/c).

If percentages are included, the functions in the last column will have to be modified. In cell L6, the formula will be:

FIGURE 22-1

```
REFERENCE STATISTICS: 1987
==================================
             Direct        Circ          Per           Micro         Ref           TOTAL
Jan                                                                                @SUM(B4..F4)
Feb                                                                                @SUM(B5..F5)
Mar                                                                                @SUM(B6..F6)
Apr                                                                                @SUM(B7..F7)
May                                                                                @SUM(B8..F8)
Jun                                                                                @SUM(B9..F9)
Jul                                                                                @SUM(B10..F10)
Aug                                                                                @SUM(B11..F11)
Sept                                                                               @SUM(B12..F12)
Oct                                                                                @SUM(B13..F13)
Nov                                                                                @SUM(B14..F14)
Dec                                                                                @SUM(B15..F15)
TOTAL        @SUM(B4..B15) @SUM(C4..C15) @SUM(D4..D15) @SUM(E4..E15) @SUM(F4..F15) @SUM(B16..F16)
```

Worksheet printed using Sideways

FIGURE 22-3

```
REFERENCE STATISTICS: 1987
==========================================================================================================================
        Directional        Circulation        Periodicals        Microforms         Reference
        Number   Percent   Number   Percent   Number   Percent   Number   Percent   Number   Percent   TOTAL
--------------------------------------------------------------------------------------------------------------------------
Jan              ERR                ERR                ERR                ERR                ERR       +B6+D6+F6+H6+J6
Feb              ERR                ERR                ERR                ERR                ERR       +B7+D7+F7+H7+J7
Mar              ERR                ERR                ERR                ERR                ERR       +B8+D8+F8+H8+J8
Apr              ERR                ERR                ERR                ERR                ERR       +B9+D9+F9+H9+J9
May              ERR                ERR                ERR                ERR                ERR       +B10+D10+F10+H10+J10
Jun              ERR                ERR                ERR                ERR                ERR       +B11+D11+F11+H11+J11
Jul              ERR                ERR                ERR                ERR                ERR       +B12+D12+F12+H12+J12
Aug              ERR                ERR                ERR                ERR                ERR       +B13+D13+F13+H13+J13
Sept             ERR                ERR                ERR                ERR                ERR       +B14+D14+F14+H14+J14
Oct              ERR                ERR                ERR                ERR                ERR       +B15+D15+F15+H15+J15
Nov              ERR                ERR                ERR                ERR                ERR       +B16+D16+F16+H16+J16
Dec              ERR                ERR                ERR                ERR                ERR       +B17+D17+F17+H17+J17
TOTAL   @SUM(B6..B17)    @SUM(D6..D17)    @SUM(F6..F17)    @SUM(H6..H17)    @SUM(J6..J17)    @SUM(L6..L17)
```

Worksheet printed using Sideways

FIGURE 22-2

```
REFERENCE STATISTICS: 1987
==========================================================================================================================
        Directional        Circulation        Periodicals        Microforms         Reference
        Number   Percent   Number   Percent   Number   Percent   Number   Percent   Number   Percent   TOTAL
--------------------------------------------------------------------------------------------------------------------------
Jan              +B6/L6             +D6/L6             +F6/L6             +H6/L6             +J6/L6
Feb              +B7/L7             +D7/L7             +F7/L7             +H7/L7             +J7/L7
Mar              +B8/L8             +D8/L8             +F8/L8             +H8/L8             +J8/L8
Apr              +B9/L9             +D9/L9             +F9/L9             +H9/L9             +J9/L9
May              +B10/L10           +D10/L10           +F10/L10           +H10/L10           +J10/L10
Jun              +B11/L11           +D11/L11           +F11/L11           +H11/L11           +J11/L11
Jul              +B12/L12           +D12/L12           +F12/L12           +H12/L12           +J12/L12
Aug              +B13/L13           +D13/L13           +F13/L13           +H13/L13           +J13/L13
Sept             +B14/L14           +D14/L14           +F14/L14           +H14/L14           +J14/L14
Oct              +B15/L15           +D15/L15           +F15/L15           +H15/L15           +J15/L15
Nov              +B16/L16           +D16/L16           +F16/L16           +H16/L16           +J16/L16
Dec              +B17/L17           +D17/L17           +F17/L17           +H17/L17           +J17/L17
TOTAL   @SUM(B6..B17)    @SUM(D6..D17)    @SUM(F6..F17)    @SUM(H6..H17)    @SUM(J6..J17)    @SUM(L6..L17)
```

Worksheet printed using Sideways

116 USING LOTUS 1-2-3

FIGURE 22-4

```
REFERENCE STATISTICS: 1987
==========================================================
        Directional                   Circulation                              Periodicals
        Number       Percent          Number        Percent                   Number        Percent
        ----------------------------------------------------------------------------------------
Jan                  @IF(@ISERR(B6/$L6),@NA,B6/$L6)     @IF(@ISERR(D6/$L6),@NA,D6/$L6)          @IF(@ISERR(F6/$L6),@NA,F6/$L6)
Feb                  @IF(@ISERR(B7/$L7),@NA,B7/$L7)     @IF(@ISERR(D7/$L7),@NA,D7/$L7)          @IF(@ISERR(F7/$L7),@NA,F7/$L7)
Mar                  @IF(@ISERR(B8/$L8),@NA,B8/$L8)     @IF(@ISERR(D8/$L8),@NA,D8/$L8)          @IF(@ISERR(F8/$L8),@NA,F8/$L8)
Apr                  @IF(@ISERR(B9/$L9),@NA,B9/$L9)     @IF(@ISERR(D9/$L9),@NA,D9/$L9)          @IF(@ISERR(F9/$L9),@NA,F9/$L9)
May                  @IF(@ISERR(B10/$L10),@NA,B10/$L10) @IF(@ISERR(D10/$L10),@NA,D10/$L10)      @IF(@ISERR(F10/$L10),@NA,F10/$L10)
Jun                  @IF(@ISERR(B11/$L11),@NA,B11/$L11) @IF(@ISERR(D11/$L11),@NA,D11/$L11)      @IF(@ISERR(F11/$L11),@NA,F11/$L11)
Jul                  @IF(@ISERR(B12/$L12),@NA,B12/$L12) @IF(@ISERR(D12/$L12),@NA,D12/$L12)      @IF(@ISERR(F12/$L12),@NA,F12/$L12)
Aug                  @IF(@ISERR(B13/$L13),@NA,B13/$L13) @IF(@ISERR(D13/$L13),@NA,D13/$L13)      @IF(@ISERR(F13/$L13),@NA,F13/$L13)
Sept                 @IF(@ISERR(B14/$L14),@NA,B14/$L14) @IF(@ISERR(D14/$L14),@NA,D14/$L14)      @IF(@ISERR(F14/$L14),@NA,F14/$L14)
Oct                  @IF(@ISERR(B15/$L15),@NA,B15/$L15) @IF(@ISERR(D15/$L15),@NA,D15/$L15)      @IF(@ISERR(F15/$L15),@NA,F15/$L15)
Nov                  @IF(@ISERR(B16/$L16),@NA,B16/$L16) @IF(@ISERR(D16/$L16),@NA,D16/$L16)      @IF(@ISERR(F16/$L16),@NA,F16/$L16)
Dec                  @IF(@ISERR(B17/$L17),@NA,B17/$L17) @IF(@ISERR(D17/$L17),@NA,D17/$L17)      @IF(@ISERR(F17/$L17),@NA,F17/$L17)
TOTAL @SUM(B6..B17)  @IF(@ISERR(B18/$L18),@NA,B18/$L18) @SUM(D6..D17) @IF(@ISERR(D18/$L18),@NA,D18/$L18)  @SUM(F6..F17) @IF(@ISERR(F18/$L18),@NA,F18/$L18)
```

Worksheet printed using Sideways

Figure 22-2
Figure 22-3

+b6+d6+f6+h6+j6

This formula is then copied down column L (/c), and Lotus will automaticallly adjust the relative cell references.

The function in the last row will be the same, but skip the percentage columns; the percentage columns should not be added.

The columns which contain the percentages should be formatted for percent (/rfp): each of the columns will have to be done individually. Then, a formula to compute the percentages will have to be written. For example, in cell C6:

+B6/$L6

This formula can be copied down the column (/c); Lotus will adjust the relative and mixed cell addresses automatically. Due to the mixed cell address ($L6), you can copy the formula to each of the percent columns; Lotus will adjust the relative address when the copy command (/c) is used. When you copy these formulas down the worksheet, you can include the last row (row 16); this will provide you with a percent for the year to date.

Unfortunately, this formula for computing percent results in a worksheet with ERR for months that have not yet been filled in; ERR is an error message. Lotus will give an error message when you attempt to divide by zero, which you will be attempting until there are values in each month of the worksheet. To avoid this error message, an @If statement can be used to compute the percentages. In cell C6, for example, use the following:

@IF(@ISERR(B6/$L6),@NA,B6/$L6)

FIGURE 22-4 Continued

	Microforms Number	Percent	Reference Number	Percent	TOTAL
		@IF(@ISERR(H6/$L6),@NA,H6/$L6)		@IF(@ISERR(J6/$L6),@NA,J6/$L6)	+B6+D6+F6+H6+J6
		@IF(@ISERR(H7/$L7),@NA,H7/$L7)		@IF(@ISERR(J7/$L7),@NA,J7/$L7)	+B7+D7+F7+H7+J7
		@IF(@ISERR(H8/$L8),@NA,H8/$L8)		@IF(@ISERR(J8/$L8),@NA,J8/$L8)	+B8+D8+F8+H8+J8
		@IF(@ISERR(H9/$L9),@NA,H9/$L9)		@IF(@ISERR(J9/$L9),@NA,J9/$L9)	+B9+D9+F9+H9+J9
		@IF(@ISERR(H10/$L10),@NA,H10/$L10)		@IF(@ISERR(J10/$L10),@NA,J10/$L10)	+B10+D10+F10+H10+J10
		@IF(@ISERR(H11/$L11),@NA,H11/$L11)		@IF(@ISERR(J11/$L11),@NA,J11/$L11)	+B11+D11+F11+H11+J11
		@IF(@ISERR(H12/$L12),@NA,H12/$L12)		@IF(@ISERR(J12/$L12),@NA,J12/$L12)	+B12+D12+F12+H12+J12
		@IF(@ISERR(H13/$L13),@NA,H13/$L13)		@IF(@ISERR(J13/$L13),@NA,J13/$L13)	+B13+D13+F13+H13+J13
		@IF(@ISERR(H14/$L14),@NA,H14/$L14)		@IF(@ISERR(J14/$L14),@NA,J14/$L14)	+B14+D14+F14+H14+J14
		@IF(@ISERR(H15/$L15),@NA,H15/$L15)		@IF(@ISERR(J15/$L15),@NA,J15/$L15)	+B15+D15+F15+H15+J15
		@IF(@ISERR(H16/$L16),@NA,H16/$L16)		@IF(@ISERR(J16/$L16),@NA,J16/$L16)	+B16+D16+F16+H16+J16
		@IF(@ISERR(H17/$L17),@NA,H17/$L17)		@IF(@ISERR(J17/$L17),@NA,J17/$L17)	+B17+D17+F17+H17+J17
	@SUM(H6..H17)	@IF(@ISERR(H18/$L18),@NA,H18/$L18)	@SUM(J6..J17)	@IF(@ISERR(J18/$L18),@NA,J18/$L18)	@SUM(L6..L17)

Worksheet printed using Sideways

Figure 22-4
Figure 22-5

This statement means: if an error message results from the division of the contents of cell B6 by the contents of cell L6, place the symbol NA (not available) in this cell. If an error message does not result from this division, divide the contents of cell B6 by the contents of cell L6. The dollar signs have been included in the references to column L to simplify the copying of the statement both down the column and then from one column to another with the copy command (/c).

FIGURE 22-5

REFERENCE STATISTICS: 1987
==============================

	Directional Number	Percent	Circulation Number	Percent	Periodicals Number	Percent	Microforms Number	Percent	Reference Number	Percent	TOTAL
Jan		NA		NA		NA		NA		NA	0
Feb		NA		NA		NA		NA		NA	0
Mar		NA		NA		NA		NA		NA	0
Apr		NA		NA		NA		NA		NA	0
May		NA		NA		NA		NA		NA	0
Jun		NA		NA		NA		NA		NA	0
Jul		NA		NA		NA		NA		NA	0
Aug		NA		NA		NA		NA		NA	0
Sept		NA		NA		NA		NA		NA	0
Oct		NA		NA		NA		NA		NA	0
Nov		NA		NA		NA		NA		NA	0
Dec		NA		NA		NA		NA		NA	0
TOTAL	0	NA	0	NA	0	NA	0	NA	0	NA	0

Worksheet printed using Sideways

23 DATABASE SEARCHING

PROBLEM
I need to keep track of the database searching performed by the librarians. Can Lotus help?

COMMANDS
Copy (/c: chapter 3)
Data query extract (/dqe: chapter 9)
Data query find (/dqf: chapter 9)
Data sort (/ds: chapter 9)
Range erase (/re: chapter 2)
Range format currency (/rfc: chapter 2)
Range format date (/rfd: chapter 2)
Range name create (/rnc: chapter 2)
Worksheet column-width set (/wcs: chapter 1)
Worksheet titles horizontal (/wth: chapter 1)

FORMULAS AND FUNCTIONS
Addition (chapter 10). @DCOUNT, @DATE, @DMIN, @DMAX, @DSUM, @IF, @SUM, and @TODAY (chapter 10)

CONCEPTS
Macros (chapter 13) and mixed and relative cell addresses (chapter 3)

Figure 23-1

Figure 23-2

To keep track of the database searching performed in a library, you can structure your worksheet in several ways. In an academic library, you would want to include columns for department and staff member's name; in a non-academic library, these columns may not be relevant. The sample worksheet will include these columns; they can be omitted in other worksheets.

The A column was headed Date; it should be formatted for date (/rfd: range format date), and the column width should be adjusted (/wcs: worksheet column-width set). The B column has been headed Dept (short for department), and the column width was adjusted (/wcs: worksheet column-width set) to 15. The C column was headed Name, and its width adjusted (/wcs: worksheet column-width set) to 20. The D column was used to record the database used and was headed DB; its width can be adjusted (/wcs: worksheet column-width set). Since BRS was used for the sample worksheet, only four-letter abbreviations are used for the databases, and the width of the column was adjusted to five. The E column was used to record the cost of the individual search; the column was formatted for currency (/rfc: range format currency) with two decimal places. The final column (F) was used to record the total spent for database searches; it was headed Total and was also formatted for currency (/rfc: range format currency) with two decimal places. The column width was adjusted (/wcs: worksheet column-width set) to allow room for large numbers.

When entering the date in the A column, you must use the @DATE function; if the current date is being recorded, use @TODAY. The information for all the other columns is simply entered as text, except for the last column (total). In this column, you need to use a formula to add the charges from the E column. In cell F2, you can simply use +E2, which copies the value from cell E2. In cell F3, use +F2+E3, which adds the value in cell F2 (total to date) to the amount for the current search (E3). This formula is then copied (/c); Lotus adjusts the cell addresses to keep the formula correct for each line.

A different way of obtaining the total to date: use the following function in cell F2:

$$@SUM(E\$2..E2)$$

When this function is copied using the copy command (/c), the row reference of the mixed cell address (E$2) will be anchored and remain the same throughout, while the relative cell address (E2) will automatically be adjusted. A running total will be obtained.

To keep the column headings on screen, use the /wth (worksheet

FIGURE 23-1

```
B1: [W15] 'Dept                                                          READY

              B               C           D         E              F
   1   Dept           Name              DB       Cost        Total
   2                                                         +E2
   3                                                         +F2+E3
   4                                                         +F3+E4
   5                                                         +F4+E5
   6                                                         +F5+E6
   7                                                         +F6+E7
   8                                                         +F7+E8
   9                                                         +F8+E9
  10                                                         +F9+E10
  11                                                         +F10+E11
  12                                                         +F11+E12
  13                                                         +F12+E13
  14                                                         +F13+E14
  15                                                         +F14+E15
  16                                                         +F15+E16
  17                                                         +F16+E17
  18                                                         +F17+E18
  19                                                         +F18+E19
  20                                                         +F19+E20
30-Nov-88   10:29 AM
```

title horizontal) command: as the screen scrolls up to permit the entering of information, the headings will remain visible. If you are not going to add any of the columns that will be described, you should do this now; otherwise, do this after the extra columns are set.

You can use additional columns to keep a running total of the amount spent on database searching for specific departments by using several @IF functions. For example, to have a running total of the searches performed for the psychology department, you can use the following function in cell G2:

@IF($B2 = "psychology", + $E2,0)

This means that if cell B2, which contains the name of the department, contains the string of characters "psychology" (quotation marks must be used), then copy the value from cell E2, which contains the cost of the individual search, and place it in this cell. If cell B2 does not contain the string of characters "psychology", place a zero here.

```
FIGURE 23-2

F2: (T) [W20] @SUM($E$2..E2)                                          READY

             C            D       E              F            G    h    I
   1  Name                DB      Cost           Total
   2                                             @SUM($E$2..E2)
   3                                             @SUM($E$2..E3)
   4                                             @SUM($E$2..E4)
   5                                             @SUM($E$2..E5)
   6                                             @SUM($E$2..E6)
   7                                             @SUM($E$2..E7)
   8                                             @SUM($E$2..E8)
   9                                             @SUM($E$2..E9)
  10                                             @SUM($E$2..E10)
  11                                             @SUM($E$2..E11)
  12                                             @SUM($E$2..E12)
  13                                             @SUM($E$2..E13)
  14                                             @SUM($E$2..E14)
  15                                             @SUM($E$2..E15)
  16                                             @SUM($E$2..E16)
  17                                             @SUM($E$2..E17)
  18                                             @SUM($E$2..E18)
  19                                             @SUM($E$2..E19)
  20                                             @SUM($E$2..E20)
  29-Mar-88  12:02 PM                                        CALC
```

Cell G3 will contain a different @IF function:

@IF($B3 = "psychology", +$E3+G2, +G2)

In other words, if cell B3 contains the string of characters "psychology", add the value from cell E3 to the value in cell G2 (the previous total for searches for the psychology department).If cell B3 does not contain the string of characters "psychology", simply copy the value from cell G2.

Since the functions contain dollar signs to make the address mixed, when they are copied using the copy command (/c) Lotus will automatically adjust only the cell addresses that need to be adjusted. As the functions are written, both horizontal and vertical copying are possible. After the function is copied horizontally, the only editing necessary will be to change the string from "psychology" to the string of characters representing the department you want to keep track of.

You can also use a similar procedure to keep track of the searches done for a particular person. In this case you change the

Figure 23-3

```
FIGURE 23-3

G1: [W40]                                                                    READY

                F                              G                    H    I    J
 1   Total
 2   @SUM($E$2..E2)        @IF($B3="psychology",$E2,0)
 3   @SUM($E$2..E3)        @IF($B4="psychology",$E3+G2,+G2)
 4   @SUM($E$2..E4)        @IF($B5="psychology",$E4+G3,+G3)
 5   @SUM($E$2..E5)        @IF($B6="psychology",$E5+G4,+G4)
 6   @SUM($E$2..E6)        @IF($B7="psychology",$E6+G5,+G5)
 7   @SUM($E$2..E7)        @IF($B8="psychology",$E7+G6,+G6)
 8   @SUM($E$2..E8)        @IF($B9="psychology",$E8+G7,+G7)
 9   @SUM($E$2..E9)        @IF($B10="psychology",$E9+G8,+G8)
10   @SUM($E$2..E10)       @IF($B11="psychology",$E10+G9,+G9)
11   @SUM($E$2..E11)       @IF($B12="psychology",$E11+G10,+G10)
12   @SUM($E$2..E12)       @IF($B13="psychology",$E12+G11,+G11)
13   @SUM($E$2..E13)       @IF($B14="psychology",$E13+G12,+G12)
14   @SUM($E$2..E14)       @IF($B15="psychology",$E14+G13,+G13)
15   @SUM($E$2..E15)       @IF($B16="psychology",$E15+G14,+G14)
16   @SUM($E$2..E16)       @IF($B17="psychology",$E16+G15,+G15)
17   @SUM($E$2..E17)       @IF($B18="psychology",$E17+G16,+G16)
18   @SUM($E$2..E18)       @IF($B19="psychology",$E18+G17,+G17)
19   @SUM($E$2..E19)       @IF($B20="psychology",$E19+G18,+G18)
20   @SUM($E$2..E20)       @IF($B21="psychology",$E20+G19,+G19)
30-Nov-88  10:30 AM                                        CALC
```

cell reference in the first part of the @IF function from B2 to C2; the string of characters (in the example "psychology") will be modified to the string of characters representing the name of the person to be tracked. In an academic library, this tracking may be useful; in a public library, it may be unorthodox, to say the least.

If you need to sort the information by department, name, or database, you can use data sort commands (/ds). To simplify the process, you can write several macros, one for each of the sorts that you will need to regularly perform.

First, you can name ranges, using range name create (/rnc):

1. sheet will be the name assigned to columns A through F of the worksheet;

2. dept will be the name assigned to the entire department column;

3. name will be the name assigned to the entire name column;

4. db will be the name assigned to the entire database column.

Using these named ranges, you can write the following macro:

'/dsdsheet˜pdept˜a˜sname˜a˜g˜

This macro selects the data sort command after obtaining a menu (/ds). The data range is sheet (dsheet˜), which is the name assigned to the entire worksheet. The primary sort key is the range named dept (pdept˜); ascending order is chosen (a˜). The secondary sort key is the range named name (sname˜), and ascending order is chosen (a˜). Lotus is then told to go ahead and sort the worksheet (g˜). The result is the worksheet sorted by department, and within department by name. This macro must be named, using the range name create command (/rnc): \d (for department) was chosen in the sample worksheet.

In a similar manner, you can write a macro to sort the worksheet by name rather than department; it is the same as the above macro except that the primary and secondary sort keys would be switched. The new macro is:

'/dsdsheet˜pname˜a˜sdept˜a˜g˜

This macro must be named: \n (for name) could be used with the range name create command (/rnc).

Furthermore, a macro to sort by database can be written. This macro would be similar to the above ones, except that the primary sort key would be db and the secondary could be either department or name. This macro is:

'/dsdsheet˜pdb˜a˜sname˜a˜g˜

In this case, the secondary sort key would be name. This macro would have to be named also, using the /rnc (range name create) command; \b (for base) was used.

In addition to data sorts, you can use data query commands. Before doing these, though, you must set up input, criterion, and output ranges. The input range refers to where Lotus is to look; the criterion range tells Lotus what to look for; the output range tells Lotus where to place the results. It is easiest to use the copy command (/c) on the row containing the column headings. These are copied to an unused portion of the worksheet for the criterion range, and then again to another unused portion of the worksheet for the output range. The copy command (/c) is used because the headings must be exactly the same in all three parts of the worksheet. Though not all the headings are necessary, and their order need not be the same, the copy command (/c) simplifies the creation of the ranges.

The input range is the entire worksheet; if you previously named the range sheet, you can use that name again.

In the criterion range, use the line under the column headings to detail exactly which records are to be chosen. For example, you can simply place one department's name under the heading dept. When you specify the criterion range, the row with the headings as well as the row(s) describing what is to be found are included. Name the criterion range criterion, using the range name create (/rnc) command.

The output range must be in an unused portion of the worksheet. Specify this range, beginning with the row containing the headings, and allow for more rows than you believe are needed for the records that Lotus will select that match your criterion. If you do not specify enough rows, Lotus will give you an error message (ERR). On the other hand, you can simply designate the row with the column headings as the output range; Lotus will then use as many rows as needed for the output. Be certain that there is nothing in the rows underneath the one line output range: Lotus will erase any information when the rows are used for the output. Name the output range output, using the range name create (/rnc) command.

Several data query commands can be performed. If you want to find specific records, the data query find (/dqf) command can be used. The input and criterion ranges must be specified before the date query find (/dqf) command is given. Lotus will then highlight the records that match the criterion selected. Using the arrow keys, each record will be highlighted in sequence.

Data query extract (/dqe) can also be performed; this command extracts all the records that match the criterion specified and places them in the output range. Before extraction can take place, input, criterion, and output ranges must be specified.

You can write a macro that will perform the data query functions of find and extract once the input range (named sheet), the criterion range (named criterion), and the output range (named output) have been named (using the /rnc, range name create, command). The first line of this macro erases the second line in the criterion range (which may have been filled in for a previous data query command), allowing the user to begin defining the criterion. The erasing is done with the following line in the macro:

'/rei4..m4~

The first character is the label prefix, which is necessary before the / in a macro; otherwise, the / will immediately cause a menu to appear. The re stands for range erase, and the i4..m4 represents the second line in the criterion range. Only the second line should be erased: the headings must be left.

Next the macro branches, using a user-defined menu:

'/xmr3˜

In other words, the left-most cell of the user-defined menu is cell R3. The menu choices are: Extract (in cell R3) and Find (in cell S3). Each of these choices is explained briefly in cells R4 and S4, respectively. Furthermore, each proceeds to slightly different macro commands.

The choice of extract leads to another user-defined menu whose left-most cell is cell R6:

'/xmr6˜

Here the user is met with the following choices: department, name, used database. (This wording is used to avoid having two choices beginning with the same letter since a choice can be made by either highlighting the desired choice and depressing the enter key or by depressing the first letter of the desired choice.) Each of these choices is explained briefly in the cells underneath.

Each of the menu choices is followed by a '/xl command:

'/xlDepartment to be found: ˜j4˜
'/xlName to be found: ˜k4˜
'/xlDatabase to be found: ˜l4˜

In each case, the information entered by the user is placed in the indicated cell, each of which is in the criterion range. More than one criterion can be specified: a user-defined menu permits the user to enter more information in the criterion range.

Finally, this portion of the macro concludes with:

'/dqisheet˜ccriterion˜ooutput˜eq
{GOTO}i9˜

The first line defines the input, criterion, and output ranges with the named ranges that were created with the range name create (/rnc) command. Lotus is then instructed to extract the records and quit the data query commands. The final line instructs Lotus to move the cursor to cell I9, which is the top line of the output range.

If you defined your output range as the single line with the column headings, this portion of the macro is finished: Lotus will automatically erase the rest of the macro range when the extract command is next invoked. If you have defined the output range as

FIGURE 23-4

```
AB1:   '/rei4..m4~
AB2:   '/xmr3~
AB3:   'Extract?
AC3:   'Find?
AB4:   'Extract records
AC4:   'Find records
AB5:   '/xmr6~
AC5:   '/xmr20~
AB6:   'Dept
AC6:   'Name
AD6:   'Used database
AB7:   'Records by department
AC7:   'Records by name
AD7:   'Records by database
AB8:   '/xlDept to be found: ~j4~
AC8:   '/xlName to be found: ~K4~
AD8:   '/xlDatabase to be found: ~l4~
AB9:   '/xmr10~
AC9:   '/xmr10~
AD9:   '/xmr10~
AB10:  'No more criterion
AC10:  'More criterion
AB11:  'No more to specify
AC11:  'Others to specify
AB12:  '/dqisheet~ccriterion~ooutput~eq
AC12:  '/xgr5~
AB13:  '{GOTO}i9~
AB14:  '/xlEnter when finished.~z1~
AB15:  '{GOTO}i10~
AB16:  '/re{END}{RIGHT}{END}{DOWN}~
AB19:  '/xmr20~
AB20:  'Dept
AC20:  'Name
AD20:  'Used database
AB21:  'Records by department
AC21:  'Records by name
AD21:  'Records by database
AB22:  '/xlDept to be found: ~j4~
AC22:  '/xlName to be found: ~K4~
AD22:  '/xlDatabase to be found: ~l4~
AB23:  '/xlOther criterion? Enter~z1~
AC23:  '/xlOther criterion? Enter~z1~
AD23:  '/xlOther criterion? Enter~z1~
AB24:  '/xmr25~
AC24:  '/xmr25~
AD24:  '/xmr25~
AB25:  'No other critierion
AC25:  'More criterion
AB26:  'Only one
AC26:  'Others to specify
AB27:  '/dqisheet~ccriterion~f
AC27:  '/xgr19~
```

Continued

```
FIGURE 23-4 Continued

AB1: '/rei4..m4~                                                              READY

                       AB                             AC
 1   /rei4..m4~
 2   /xmr3~
 3   Extract?                          Find?
 4   Extract records                   Find records
 5   /xmr6~                            /xmr20~
 6   Dept                              Name
 7   Records by department             Records by name
 8   /xlDept to be found: ~j4~         /xlName to be found: ~K4~
 9   /xmr10~                           /xmr10~
10   No more criterion                 More criterion
11   No more to specify                Others to specify
12   /dqisheet~ccriterion~ooutput~e/xgr5~
13   {GOTO}i9~
14   /xlEnter when finished.~z1~
15   {GOTO}i10~
16   /re{END}{RIGHT}{END}{DOWN}~
17
18
19   /xmr20~
20   Dept                              Name
02-Dec-88  10:01 AM
```

more than one line, you must erase the entire output except for the column headings. To do this, a few more lines are necessary.

First, an /xl command posts the following message: Enter when finished. After examining the output, depress the enter key. Lotus then takes the following actions:

{GOTO}i10˜
'/re{END}{RIGHT}{END}{DOWN}˜

This sequence moves the cursor to the second line of the output range and erases the entire output range except for the column headings. Thus the output range is prepared for the next data query extract.

If the original menu choice was find rather than extract, the macro continues operation in another cell. In this case, cell R20 was used. Here the same sort of menu is provided, allowing the user to define the criterion by name, department, and/or database. The final line in this case is:

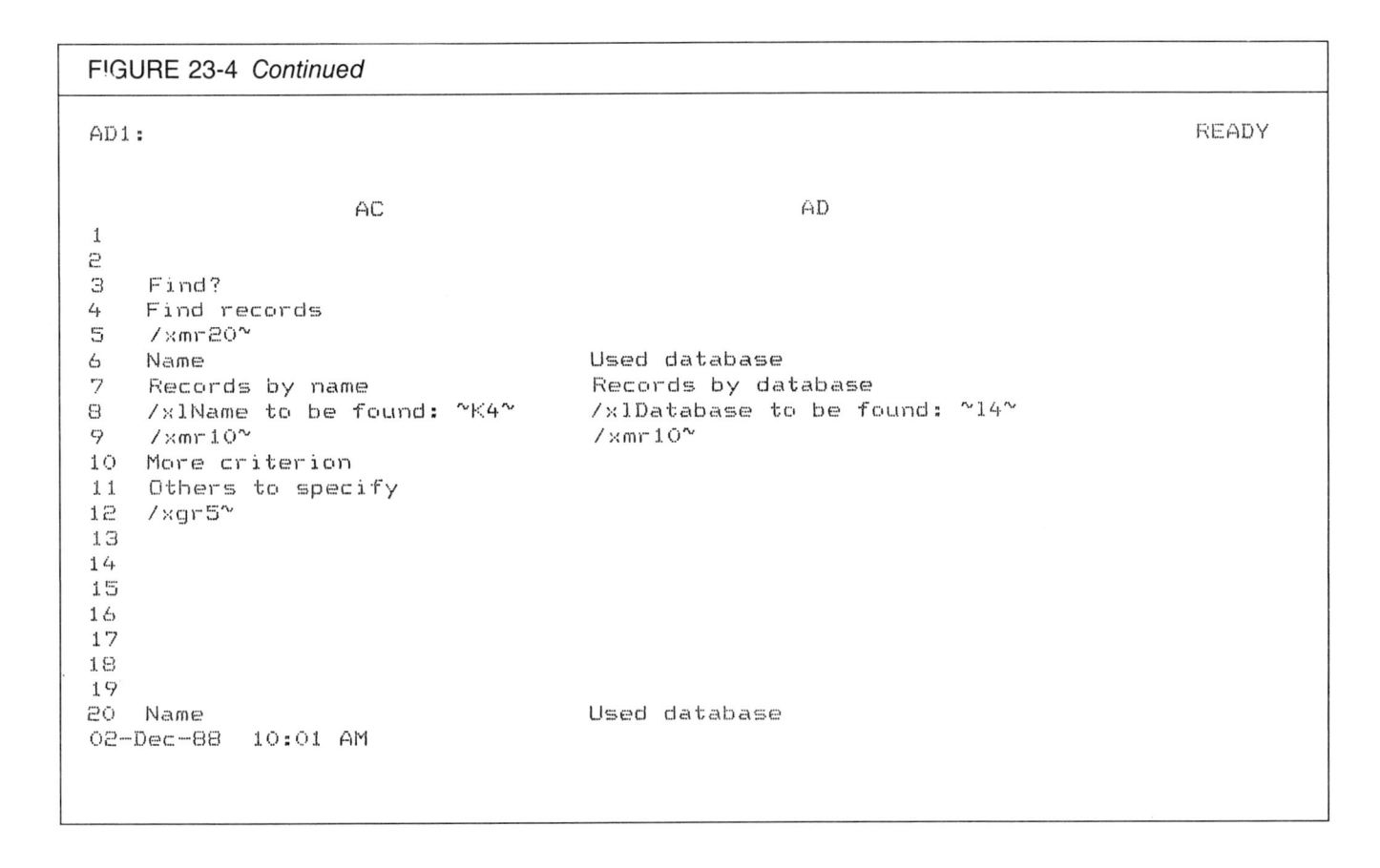

FIGURE 23-4 Continued

```
AD1:                                                              READY


                 AC                             AD
 1
 2
 3    Find?
 4    Find records
 5    /xmr20~
 6    Name                       Used database
 7    Records by name            Records by database
 8    /xlName to be found: ~K4~  /xlDatabase to be found: ~I4~
 9    /xmr10~                    /xmr10~
10    More criterion
11    Others to specify
12    /xgr5~
13
14
15
16
17
18
19
20    Name                       Used database
02-Dec-88  10:01 AM
```

Figure 23-4

'/dqisheet˜ccriterion˜f

An output range does not have to be specified for the data query find (/dqf) command. With this command, Lotus simply highlights in the input range the records that match the stated criterion.

It is possible to use database statistical functions on this database. These functions, incorporated into a macro, will automatically provide the following information for records that match user-defined criterion: total amount spent (@DSUM), average amount (@DAVG), maximum (@DMAX) and minimum (@DMIN) costs, and a count (@DCOUNT) of the number of items.

First, copy the criterion range column headings to a blank portion of the worksheet using the copy command (/c). In the example, this information was copied to cell AA26. This will form the top of the chart, which will contain the results of the database statistical functions. The first and second lines of the macro erase the information in the second line of the database statistical table as well as in the second line of the criterion range.

FIGURE 23-4 *Continued*

```
AB28:                                                                    READY

                    AB                              AC
 19  /xmr20~
 20  Dept                               Name
 21  Records by department              Records by name
 22  /xlDept to be found: ~j4~          /xlName to be found: ~K4~
 23  /xlOther criterion? Enter~z1~      /xlOther criterion? Enter~z1~
 24  /xmr25~                            /xmr25~
 25  No other critierion                More criterion
 26  Only one                           Others to specify
 27  /dqisheet~ccriterion~f             /xgr19~
 28
 29
 30
 31
 32
 33
 34
 35
 36
 37
 38
02-Dec-88  10:02 AM
```

'/reaa28..ac28~
'/rei4..m4~

Then an '/xl command posts the message: Define criterion. Enter. When the enter key is depressed, a user-defined menu is presented, permitting the user to select the criterion. The user-provided information is placed in the appropriate cells in the criterion range. For example, the following is used:

'/xlName to be found: ~k4~

This places the name provided by the user in cell K4. More than one criterion can be defined, as the user is permitted to return to the menu to provide more than one. The information is then copied to the second line of the database statistical table to aid the user in understanding exactly what the results mean.

The last two lines of the macro are:

{CALC}~
{GOTO}AA26~

As Lotus does not automatically recalculate the results of the database statistical functions, it is important that the macro provide the {CALC} line. The final line moves the cursor to the indicated cell. The entire table, including the lines defining the specified criterion, is displayed.

Figure 23-5

FIGURE 23-5

```
/reaa28..ac28~
/rei4..m4~
/xlDefine criterion. Enter~z1~
/xmab5~
a. Name                          b. Department                    c. Database
Specify name                     Specify department               Specify database
/xlName to be found: ~k4~        /xlDpeartment to be found: ~j4~  /xlDatabase to be found: ~l4~
/ck4~ab28~                       /cj4~aa28~                       /cl4~ac28~
/xmab10~                         /xmab10~                         /xmab10~
No more                          More
Finished specifying              Specify more
{CALC}~                          /xgab4~
{GOTO}aa26~
```

Worksheet printed using Sideways

24 SOFTWARE EVALUATION

PROBLEM
I want to introduce bibliographic instruction software into my library, but I have no way of evaluating the available programs. Can Lotus help?

COMMANDS
Copy (/c: chapter 3)
File save (/fs: chapter 6)
Print printer (/pp: chapter 7)
Range name create (/rnc: chapter 2)
Worksheet column display (/wcd: chapter 1)
Worksheet column hide (/wch: chapter 1)
Worksheet erase (/we: chapter 1)

FORMULAS AND FUNCTIONS
Division and multiplication (chapter 10), @IF, and @SUM (chapter 10)

CONCEPTS
Macros (chapter 13) and relative cell addresses (chapter 3)

Figure 24-1
Figure 24-2

Using Lotus 1-2-3, it is possible to set up an evaluation form for this function as well as others. Briefly, this form asks for evaluative information on a number of different points, weights the responses, and produces a percentage figure that can be used to compare different software as well as different reviewers' responses. After the entire form is filled out, a summary is printed, which includes the reviewer's name, program name, equipment required, and percentage. Finally, it asks the user if the entire worksheet should be saved or, if the summary is enough, erased.

The key to setting up this evaluation form is a macro that uses {GETNUMBER} and {GETLABEL}. If you are using an earlier release of Lotus, the commands are /xn and /xl. Both of these permit the person setting up the form to have textual information displayed in the control panel (the top portion of the screen) and permit the user to input responses in specified locations. The following is an example of these commands:

{GETLABEL "Reviewer's name, ",K3}~

Or (in the older releases):

'/xlReviewer's name: ~k3~

In the control panel, Lotus will display the message—Reviewer's name—and then pause for input from the user. The input will be recorded in the designated cell, K3, when the enter key is depressed. In a similar manner, the command {GETNUMBER} is used as follows:

{GETNUMBER "Operating time (0-5): ",c17}~

Or, in the earlier releases of Lotus:

'/xnOperating time (0-5): ~c17~

In the control panel, the indicated message Operating time (0-5): is displayed. Lotus then pauses, waiting for input. The user's response is then recorded in the designated cell, C17, when the enter key is depressed.

The difference between the newer and older releases of Lotus should be noted with care. The newer releases use braces to surround the entire macro command; the older releases do not. Furthermore, the text to be displayed in the control panel in the

130

SOFTWARE EVALUATION

FIGURE 24-1

```
B1:  [W77] '{GETLABEL "General: Press enter to continue",c1}~
B2:  [W77] '{GETLABEL "Reviewer's Name: ",k2}~
B3:  [W77] '{GETLABEL "Program name: ",k3}~
B4:  [W77] '{GETLABEL "Release (number or date): ",k4}~
B5:  [W77] '{GETLABEL "Equipment requiremnets: Press enter to continue",c5}~
B6:  [W77] '{GETLABEL "Computer: ",k5}~
B7:  [W77] '{MENUBRANCH b8}
B8:  [W77] 'Available
B9:  [W77] 'Computer available or obtainable
B10: [W77] '{GETLABEL "Disk drives needed: ",k6}~
B11: [W77] '{GETLABEL "Monitor type required: ",k7}~
B12: [W77] '{GETLABEL "Peripherals required: ",k8}~
B13: [W77] '{GETLABEL "For each as indicated, rate program 0-5; enter to con
tinue",c13}~
B14: [W77] '{GETNUMBER "Turnkey/self-booting system (0-5): ",c14}~
B15: [W77] '{GETLABEL "Time requirements; Press enter to continue",c15}~
B16: [W77] '{GETNUMBER "Booting time (0-5): ",c16}~
B17: [W77] '{GETNUMBER "Operating time (0-5): ",c17}~
B18: [W77] '{GETLABEL "Supplementary materials provided: Press enter to cont
inue",c18}~
B19: [W77] '{GETNUMBER "Documentation (0-5) ",c19}~
B20: [W77] '{GETNUMBER "Library Guide (0-5): ",c20}~
B21: [W77] '{GETLABEL "Problem handling provisions; Enter to continue",c21}~
B22: [W77] '{GETNUMBER "Hotline for help available (0-5): ",c22}~
B23: [W77] '{GETNUMBER "Replacement availability (0-5): ",c23}~
B24: [W77] '{GETLABEL "For each as indicated, rate program 0-5; Enter to con
tinue",c24}~
B25: [W77] '/xg\b~
B27: [W77] '{GETLABEL "Program content; Enter to continue",c27}~
B28: [W77] '{GETNUMBER "Aims/objectives stated (0-5): ",c28}~
B29: [W77] '{GETNUMBER "Aims/objectives clear (0-5): ",c29}~
B30: [W77] '{GETNUMBER "Aims/objectives have educational significance (0-5):
 ",c30}~
B31: [W77] '{GETNUMBER "Aims/objectives obtainable (0-5): ",c31}~
B32: [W77] '{GETNUMBER "Aims/objectives match library's needs (0-5): ",c32}~
B33: [W77] '{GETNUMBER "Aims/objectives match curriculum (0-5): ",c33}~
B34: [W77] '{GETNUMBER "Teaching philosophy matches program methods (0-5): "
,c34}~
B35: [W77] '{GETNUMBER "Prerequisite reading skills appropriate (0-5): ",c35
}~
B36: [W77] '{GETNUMBER "Prerequisite skills/knowledge appropriate (0-5): ",c
36}~
B37: [W77] '{GETNUMBER "Prerequisite language level appropriate (0-5): ",c37
}~
B38: [W77] '{GETNUMBER "Useable in a variety of situations (0-5): ",c38}~
B39: [W77] '{GETNUMBER "Good educational practices followed (0-5): ",c39}~
B40: [W77] '{GETLABEL "For each of the indicated, rate program 0-5; Enter to
 continue",c40}~
B41: [W77] '{GETNUMBER "Factually accurate (0-5): ",c41}~
B42: [W77] '{GETNUMBER "Free of biases and stereotypes (0-5): ",c42}~
B43: [W77] '{GETNUMBER "Knowledge gained transferable (0-5): ",c43}~
B44: [W77] '/xg\c~
```

Continued

FIGURE 24-1 Continued

```
B46: [W77] '{GETLABEL "Presentation; Enter to continue",c46}~
B47: [W77] '{GETNUMBER "Personalized (0-5): ",c47}~
B48: [W77] '{GETNUMBER "Directions clear (0-5): ",c48}~
B49: [W77] '{GETNUMBER "Directions on screen or accessible (0-5): ",c49}~
B50: [W77] '{GETNUMBER "Format clear and consistant (0-5) ",c50}~
B51: [W77] '{GETLABEL "Screen displays: Enter to continue",c51}~
B52: [W77] '{GETNUMBER "Effective screen displays (0-5) ",c52}~
B53: [W77] '{GETNUMBER "Screen spacing attractive (0-5) ",c53}~
B54: [W77] '{GETNUMBER "Text clear and atttractive (0-5): ",c54}~
B55: [W77] '{GETNUMBER "Print size and type adequate (0-5): ",c55}~
B56: [W77] '{GETNUMBER "Color used effectively (0-5): ",c56}~
B57: [W77] '{GETNUMBER "Animation used effectively (0-5): ",c57}~
B58: [W77] '{GETNUMBER "Graphics used effectively (0-5): ",c58}~
B59: [W77] '{GETNUMBER "Sound used effectively (0-5): ",c59}~
B60: [W77] '{GETNUMBER "Material is organized and logical (0-5): ",c60}~
B61: [W77] '{GETNUMBER "For each as indicated, rate program 0-5",c61}
B62: [W77] '/xg\d~
B64: [W77] '{GETLABEL "Experience of using program; Enter to continue",c64}~
B65: [W77] '{GETNUMBER "Pleasant/enjoyable experience (0-5): ",c65}~
B66: [W77] '{GETNUMBER "Interesting experience (0-5): ",c66}~
B67: [W77] '{GETNUMBER "Motivating experience (0-5): ",c67}~
B68: [W77] '{GETNUMBER "Stimulates creativity (0-5): ",c68}~
B69: [W77] '{GETLABEL "Interaction/use of computer; Enter to continue",c69}~
B70: [W77] '{GETNUMBER "User friendly (0-5): ",c70}~
B71: [W77] '{GETNUMBER "Control keys used consistantly (0-5): ",c71}~
B72: [W77] '{GETNUMBER "User able to control pace (0-5): ",c72}~
B73: [W77] '{GETNUMBER "User able to enter at different levels and places (0-5): ",c73}~
B74: [W77] '{GETNUMBER "User able to save results and restart (0-5) ",c74}~
B75: [W77] '{GETNUMBER "User able to control sequence (0-5): ",c75}~
B76: [W77] '{GETNUMBER "Active user involvement (0-5) ",c76}~
B77: [W77] '/xg\e~
B79: [W77] '{GETLABEL "Responses: Enter to continue",c79}~
B80: [W77] '{GETNUMBER "Prompting/need for input signalled (0-5): ",c80}~
B81: [W77] '{GETNUMBER "Time/number of attempts limited (0-5) ",c81}~
B82: [W77] '{GETNUMBER "Accepts various input types (0-5): ",c82}~
B83: [W77] '{GETNUMBER "Abbreviations accepted (0-5): ",c83}~
B84: [W77] '{GETNUMBER "Synonyms accepted (0-5): ",c84}~
B85: [W77] '{GETNUMBER "Open-ended resposes permitted (0-5): ",c85}~
B86: [W77] '{GETNUMBER "Positive feedback (0-5): ",c86}~
B87: [W77] '{GETNUMBER "Positive reinforcement (0-5) ",c87}~
B88: [W77] '{GETNUMBER "Branching capability (0-5) ",c88}~
B89: [W77] '{GETNUMBER "Help available (0-5): ",c89}~
B90: [W77] '{GETNUMBER "Definitions and explanations available (0-5): ",c90}
B91: [W77] '{GETNUMBER "Easy exit and restart (0-5): ",c91}~
B92: [W77] '{GETNUMBER "Independence from librarian intervention (0-5): ",c923~
B93: [W77] '{GETLABEL "Librarian's use: Enter to continue",c93}~
B94: [W77] '{GETNUMBER "Modifiable/expandable (0-5): ",c94}~
B95: [W77] '{GETNUMBER "Record keeping possible (0-5): ",c95}~
B96: [W77] '{GETNUMBER "Printout available (0-5): ",c96}~
B97: [W77] '{GETLABEL "Turn printer on, then enter",c97}~
B98: [W77] '/xg\z~
```

Continued

SOFTWARE EVALUATION   133

FIGURE 24-2

```
B1:  [W77] '/x1General: Press enter to continue ~c1~
B2:  [W77] '/x1Reviewer's name: ~k2~
B3:  [W77] '/x1Program name: ~k3~
B4:  [W77] '/x1Release (number or date): ~k4~
B5:  [W77] '/x1Equipment required: Enter ~c5~
B6:  [W77] '/x1Computer: ~k5~
B7:  [W77] '/xmb8~
B8:  [W77] 'Available
B9:  [W77] 'Computer available or obtainable
B10: [W77] '/x1Disk drives needed: ~k6~
B11: [W77] '/x1Monitor type needed: ~k7~
B12: [W77] '/x1Peripherals required: ~k8~
B13: [W77] '/x1As indicated, rate program 0-5: Enter ~c13~
B14: [W77] '/xnTurnkey/self booting system (0-5): ~c14~
B15: [W77] '/x1Time requirements: Enter ~c15~
B16: [W77] '/xnBooting time (0-5): ~c16~
B17: [W77] '/xnOperating time (0-5): ~c17~
B18: [W77] '/x1Supplementary materials provided: Enter ~c18~
B19: [W77] '/xnDocumentation (0-5): ~c19~
B20: [W77] '/xnLibrary guide (0-5): ~c20~
B21: [W77] '/x1Problem handling provisions: Enter ~c21~
B22: [W77] '/xnHotline for help available (0-5): ~c22~
B23: [W77] '/xnReplacement availability (0-5): ~c23~
B24: [W77] '/x1As indicated, rate program 0-5: Enter ~c24~
B25: [W77] '/xg\b~
B27: [W77] '/x1Program content: Enter ~c27~
B28: [W77] '/xnAims/objectives stated (0-5): ~c28~
B29: [W77] '/xnAims/objectives clear (0-5): ~c29~
B30: [W77] '/xnAims: educationally significant (0-5): ~c30~
B31: [W77] '/xnAims/objectives obtainable (0-5): ~c31~
B32: [W77] '/xnAims match library needs (0-5): ~c32~
B33: [W77] '/xnAims match curriculum (0-5): ~c33~
B34: [W77] '/xnTeach phil matches program (0-5): ~c34~
B35: [W77] '/xnPrerequisite reading skills (0-5): ~c35~
B36: [W77] '/xnPrerequisite knowledge/skills (0-5): ~c36~
B37: [W77] '/xnPrerequisite language level (0-5): ~c37~
B38: [W77] '/xnUseable in many situations (0-5) ~c38~
B39: [W77] '/xnGood educational practices (0-5): ~c39~
B40: [W77] '/x1As indicated, rate program 0-5 ~c40~
B41: [W77] '/xnFactually accurate (0-5): ~c41~
B42: [W77] '/xnNo bias or stereotype (0-5): ~c42~
B43: [W77] '/xnTransferable knowledge (0-5): ~c43~
B44: [W77] '/xg\c~
B46: [W77] '/x1Presentation: Enter ~c46~
B47: [W77] '/xnPersonalized (0-5): ~c47~
B48: [W77] '/xnDirections clear (0-5): ~c48~
```

Continued

newer releases is surrounded by quotation marks. The cell location designation is surrounded by ~ in the older releases. The releases

FIGURE 24-2 Continued

```
B49: [W77] '/xnDirections on screen/accessible (0-5): ~c49~
B50: [W77] '/xnFormat clear/consistant (0-5): ~c50~
B51: [W77] '/xlScreen displays: Enter ~c51~
B52: [W77] '/xnEffective screen displays (0-5): ~c52~
B53: [W77] '/xnScreen spacing attractive (0-5): ~c53~
B54: [W77] '/xnText clear/attractive (0-5): ~c54~
B55: [W77] '/xnPrint size/type adequate (0-5): ~c55~
B56: [W77] '/xnColor used effectively (0-5): ~c56~
B57: [W77] '/xnAnimation used effectively (0-5): ~c57~
B58: [W77] '/xnGraphics used effectively (0-5): ~c58~
B59: [W77] '/xnSound used effectively (0-5): ~c59~
B60: [W77] '/xnMaterial: Organized/logical (0-5): ~c60~
B61: [W77] '/xlAs indicated, rate program 0-5: Enter ~c61~
B62: [W77] '/xg\d~
B64: [W77] '/xlExperience of using program: Enter ~c64~
B65: [W77] '/xnPleasant/enjoyable experience (0-5): ~c65~
B66: [W77] '/xnInteresting experience (0-5): ~c66~
B67: [W77] '/xnMotivating experience (0-5): ~c67~
B68: [W77] '/xnStimulates creativity (0-5): ~c68~
B69: [W77] '/xlInteraction/use of computer: Enter ~c69~
B70: [W77] '/xnUser friendly (0-5): ~c70~
B71: [W77] '/xnControl keys used consistantly (0-5): ~c71~
B72: [W77] '/xnUser can control pace (0-5): ~c72~
B73: [W77] '/xnEnter at many levels/places (0-5): ~c73~
B74: [W77] '/xnCan save results and restart (0-5): ~c74~
B75: [W77] '/xnCan control sequence (0-5): ~c75~
B76: [W77] '/xnActive user involvement (0-5): ~c76~
B77: [W77] '/xg\e~
B79: [W77] '/xlResponses: Enter ~c79~
B80: [W77] '/xnPrompting/input need signalled (0-5): ~c80~
B81: [W77] '/xnTime/attempts limited (0-5): ~c81~
B82: [W77] '/xnAccepts many input types (0-5): ~c82~
B83: [W77] '/xnAbbreviations accepted (0-5): ~c83~
B84: [W77] '/xnSynonyms accepted (0-5): ~c84~
B85: [W77] '/xnPermits open-ended responses (0-5): ~c85~
B86: [W77] '/xnPositive feedback (0-5): ~c86~
B87: [W77] '/xnPositive reinforcement (0-5): ~c87~
B88: [W77] '/xnBranching capability (0-5): ~c88~
B89: [W77] '/xnHelp available (0-5): ~c89~
B90: [W77] '/xnExplanations available (0-5): ~c90~
B91: [W77] '/xnEasy exit and restart (0-5): ~c91~
B92: [W77] '/xnIndependant operation (0-5): ~c92~
B93: [W77] '/xlLibrarian's use: Enter ~c93~
B94: [W77] '/xnModifiable/expandable (0-5): ~c94~
B95: [W77] '/xnRecord keeping possible (0-5): ~c95~
B96: [W77] '/xnPrintout available (0-5): ~c96~
B97: [W77] '/xlTurn printer on; then enter ~c97~
B98: [W77] '/xg\z~
```

that use '/xl and '/xn permit fewer characters for textual messages than those that use {GETLABEL} and {GETNUMBER}. On the other hand, '/xn will only accept a number: if anything else is entered, Lotus will beep and show an error message (ERR).

This form requests the evaluator the rate each of the points from 0 to 5. If a number higher than 5 is recorded in column C, the function in column H tells Lotus to record 5, and if the number is less than 5, to record that number. The following @IF function accomplishes this:

$$@IF(c14>5,5,C14)$$

This function is then copied, using the copy command (/c). Lotus adjusts all the cell relative addresses.

The possibly adjusted values are then multiplied by the weighted values, which are filled in before the form is used, depending on the library's needs and philosophy. For example, the use of sound may not be considered as relevant for a library where the microcomputer must be in the center of the reference area due to space restrictions. In this case, the answer would probably be weighted as

Figure 24-3

FIGURE 24-3

```
H31: @IF(C31>5,5,C31)                                              READY


           F                    G                    H
12
13
14    +H14*E14              5*E14                @IF(C14>5,5,C14)
15    +H15*E15              5*E15                @IF(C15>5,5,C15)
16    +H16*E16              5*E16                @IF(C16>5,5,C16)
17    +H17*E17              5*E17                @IF(C17>5,5,C17)
18                                               @IF(C18>0,0,0)
19    +H19*E19              5*E19                @IF(C19>5,5,C19)
20    +H20*E20              5*E20                @IF(C20>5,5,C20)
21                                               @IF(C21>0,0,0)
22    +H22*E22              5*E22                @IF(C22>5,5,C22)
23    +H23*E23              5*E23                @IF(C23>5,5,C23)
24                                               @IF(C24>0,0,0)
25
26
27                                               @IF(C27>0,0,0)
28    +H28*E28              5*E28                @IF(C28>5,5,C28)
29    +H29*E29              5*E29                @IF(C29>5,5,C29)
30    +H30*E30              5*E30                @IF(C30>5,5,C30)
31    +H31*E31              5*E31                @IF(C31>5,5,C31)
30-Nov-88   10:33 AM
```

0. The weighted totals are then added together (using the function @SUM(H14..H97) and divided by the highest possible score.

When you study the macro, you will see that the text is divided into several separate macros. This has been done to permit separate portions of the macro to be tested separately before linking them together with /xg, which instructs Lotus to continue execution with the macro that then follows. (For example, after \a has been completed, the macro instructs Lotus to continue execution at the macro named \b by using the following line: '/xg\b~.)

Each of the macros must be named, using the /rnc (range name create) command. If the cursor is on the first line of the macro being named, you can simply depress the enter key in response to the range, since only the first line of a macro needs to be specified.

The command {MENUBRANCH}, which in the older releases of Lotus is /xm, is also used in this macro. {MENUBRANCH} creates a user-defined menu at a specified point in the macro. It permits user intervention in allowing a choice as to actions. In the first case that the command is used, the user has just been asked for the type of computer required for use with the program being evaluated. Then:

{MENUBRANCH B8}

Or, for those using an older release of Lotus:

'/xmB8~

This line instructs Lotus to look in cell B8 for the beginning of the user-defined menu to be displayed in the control panel. At B8 through C9 are the following:

Available	Not Available
Computer available or obtainable	Quit

The choice between Available and Not Available can be made as any of the regular menu choices can be made: either move the highlighter to the appropriate choice by using the arrow keys and then depress the enter key, or depress the first letter of the choice (in this case either A or N). As with the other Lotus menus, the choices are displayed, as are brief explanations; in this case cells B9 and C9 contain the explanations. These cells do not have to be specified in the {MENUBRANCH} command: the cells directly under the menu choices are automatically displayed when the {MENUBRACH} or /xm command is executed.

Finally, the {MENUBRANCH} command divides the macro into separate routes, one for each of the choices; in this case, the first choice (Available) continues operation of the macro down the B column. The other choice (Not Available) continues in the C column with the command '/q (quit), which ends the evaluation process.

At the end of column B, the macro is instructed to continue operation at the macro named \z ('/xg\z~), where the percentage of the possible score is copied to cell K9 using the following formula:

'/cc105~k9~

This means copy the contents of cell C105 to cell K9. Then the printing commands are issued as part of the macro:

'/pprj1..k9~gpq

This line instructs Lotus to select the print option from the main menu (/p), choose printer (p), define the range as J1 to K9 (r), print (g which stands for go), move the paper in the printer to the top of the page (p), and then quit the print menu (q).

The macro then proceeds to another {MENUBRANCH} or /xm:

{MENUBRANCH p1} or '/xmP1~

Beginning in cell P1, the following menu appears:

Column P	Column Q
Save	Quit
Save work	Do not save
'/fs(?)~	'/wey

Column P (Save) instructs Lotus to call up the main menu, select file, select save, and then pause for the user to supply a name for the file to be saved under. Column Q instructs Lotus to call up the main menu, select worksheet, select erase, and confirm the choice. The worksheet will then be erased from the machine's memory. The original file is still on the disk, ready for the next evaluator.

After the entire form has been tested and works correctly, one further modification should be made: the creation of a \0 macro. This macro will automatically execute any time the file is loaded. Without using a \0 macro, the user would have to know how to begin macro operation.

Figure 24-4

```
FIGURE 24-4

K1:                                                                    READY

            I             J             K       L         M      N       O
    1                 SUMMARY:                \z
    2                 Reviewer's Name:        /cc105~k9~
    3                 Program Name:           /pprj1..k9~gpq
    4                 Release:                {MENUBRANCH p1}
    5                 Computer:
    6                 Disk Drives:
    7                 Monitor:
    8                 Peripherals:
    9                 Percent:
   10
   11
   12
   13
   14
   15
   16
   17
   18
   19
   20
   30-Nov-88   10:33 AM
```

The \0 macro used with this form is as follows:

'{MENUBRANCH q10} or '/xmq10~
Evaluate   Prepare
Fill in form   Get form ready
'/xg\a~

The first selection (Evaluate) instructs Lotus to proceed to the macro entitled \a, which is the beginning of the form. The second selection (Prepare) does not begin macro execution. Instead, it permits the user the opportunity to edit the form, assign weighted values, etc. In the later releases of Lotus, this \0 macro should be modified one more time: a line should be added at the beginning:

Figure 24-5

'/wcha1..s100~

This line will hide the entire worksheet from the view of the evaluator: this will reduce the confusion by having the entire screen

```
FIGURE 24-5

P1: 'Save                                                                    READY


               P                      Q                  R
  1   Save                    Quit
  2   Save worksheet          Do not save
  3   /fs{?}~                 /wey
  4
  5
  6
  7
  8   \0                      /wcha1..s100~
  9                           {MENUBRANCH q10}
 10                           Evaluate           Prepare
 11                           Fill in form       Get form ready
 12                           /xg\a~             /wcda1..s100~
 13
 14
 15
 16
 17
 18
 19
 20
 30-Nov-88   10:34 AM
```

blank except for the control panel. This is accomplished by calling for the menu (/), selecting worksheet (w), column-width (c), and hide (h). Then the range to be hidden is selected. Of course, if this is added, it is necessary to add one further line to the second column of this \0 macro: if the user chooses to prepare the worksheet rather than evaluate, the worksheet should be fully displayed. This is accomplished by using the following line:

'/wcda1..s100˜

This line is similar to the one that hides the entire worksheet, except that instead of hide, display has been chosen.

25 SHELVING

PROBLEM
I need a way to train shelvers. Can Lotus help?

COMMANDS
Data fill (/df: chapter 9)
Data sort (/ds: chapter 9)
File retrieve (/fr: chapter 6)
Range input (/ri: chapter 2)
Move (/m: chapter 4)
Range name create (/rnc: chapter 2)
Range protect (/rp: chapter 2)
Worksheet column hide (/wch: chapter 1)
Worksheet column-width set (/wcs: chapter 1)

CONCEPTS
Macros (chapter 13)

Lotus can help to train shelvers. It does this by enabling the shelvers to practice placing call numbers in order. Then the chosen order can be checked by Lotus, and various help messages can be displayed. Additionally, Lotus can reload the worksheet automatically until all of the mistakes have been eliminated.

To teach shelving, the Lotus worksheet should be divided into three parts:

1. The first part is the one that the shelvers will see;
2. The second part contains the macros;
3. The third part contains the messages which will be displayed to aid the shelvers in understanding their mistakes.

The first part of the worksheet contains what the shelvers will see. The first few lines should be filled with instructions, such as:

Place the following call numbers in order:
Number column B from 1 to 10
Then depress Alt and C together

The last line invokes a macro which will be explained later.

Then, skipping a few lines and leaving columns A and B blank, ten call numbers are entered. Use two cells in adjacent columns for each call number. The break should be where the decimal point occurs. Since Lotus was not designed for the purpose for which it is being used in this case, a label prefix (such as ') must be placed before the decimal point. Otherwise, Lotus will automatically place a zero in front of the decimal point.

The ten call numbers that have been used in the example are:

Column C	Column D
PQ 77	.49 D 3 1987
P 355	.7 F 3667 1977
PA 3	.1 Z 8 1945
P 355	.68 F 3667 1978
PZ 1	.14 P 1976
PQ 8	.14 E 22 1986
PZ 1	.123 P 1974
PZ 1	.123 P 1975
PA 3	.12 Z 2 1945
PZ 1	.2 P 1973

Figure 25-1

Of course, the width of the D column should be adjusted to accommodate the length of the call numbers; /wcs (worksheet column-width set) is used.

Once the user has numbered the call numbers one to ten in column B, s/he invokes a macro by depressing Alt and C simultaneously. This macro does several things:

'/dsrdb5..d14˜pc5..c14˜a˜sd5..d14˜a˜g

This calls up the menu (/), selects data sort (ds), resets the settings (r) and defines the range as B5 to D14 (dsrdb5..d14). The primary sort key is C5 to C14 (pc5..c14˜), and ascending order is chosen (a˜). The secondary sort key is D5 to D14 and ascending order is once again selected (sd5..d14˜a˜). Finally, the sorting is done by instructing Lotus to go (g).

In each cell, Lotus looks at one character at a time to sort. Unfortunately, this creates a problem for librarians: PQ 77 will be placed before PQ 8. In the macro, this has to be corrected. One way to correct this is by using the move command:

```
FIGURE 25-1

F1:                                                              READY


         A         B         C         D         E        F        G        H
 1   Place the following call numbers in order:
 2   Number column B 1 to 10, then
 3   Depress Alt and C
 4
 5                       PQ 77     .49 D 3 1987
 6                       P 355     .7 F 3667 1977
 7                       PA 3      .1 Z 2 1945
 8                       P 355     .68 F 3667 1978
 9                       PZ 1      .14 P 1976
10                       PQ 8      .14 E 22 1986
11                       PZ 1      .123 P 1974
12                       PZ 1      .123 P 1975
13                       PA 3      .12 Z 2 1945
14                       PZ 1      .2 P1973
15
16
17
18
19
20
30-Mar-88  09:00 AM
```

'/mb9..d9~b4~
'/mb10..d10~b9~
'/mb4..d4~b10~

This series of commands moves the entry from cells B9 through D9 to an unoccupied set of cells (B4 to D4), then moves the entry from cells B10 through D10 to cells B9 through D9, and finally moves the entry from cells B4 through D4 to cells B10 through D10. In other words, the positions of the entries have been reversed.

The macro continues:

'/dfa5..a14~1~1~10~

This line tells Lotus to get the menu (/), select data fill (df) in cells A5 to A14 starting from 1 (1~) using a step of 1 (1~) and ending at 10 (10~). This command will cause Lotus to number the entries from 1 to 10 once they have been sorted into the correct order.

The macro continues with a message:

{GETLABEL "Check columns A (correct) and B (yours). Then enter",m1}~

This line displays the message indicated by quotation marks. If you are using an earlier release of Lotus, it is possible to use the /xl command, though the number of characters in the message will be restricted. The {GETLABEL} command requires the use of a cell location at the end. In this case, an empty cell was chosen (cell M1).

When the user depresses the enter key, Lotus continues the macro with a series of /xi commands:

'/xib5=2#and#b6=1~/xg\a~
'/xg\h~

In other words, if cell B5 equals 2 and cell B6 equals 1, continue operating by going to \a, another macro. The error in this case would be that the user did not understand the use of a decimal point. The message contained in \a utilizes several {GETLABEL} commands as follows:

{GETLABEL "After the decimal, add zeroes; then put in order. Enter",aa3}~
{GETLABEL "After the decimal, zeroes do not change the number. Enter",aa4}~
{GETLABEL "Try again. Enter",aa5}~

Figure 25-2

FIGURE 25-2

```
F4:                                                              READY


          A           B         C          D         E       F       G       H
 1  Place the following call numbers in order:
 2  Number column B 1 to 10, then
 3  Depress Alt and C
 4
 5            1         2 P 355    .68 F 3667 1978
 6            2         1 P 355    .7 F 3667 1977
 7            3         3 PA 3     .1 Z 2 1945
 8            4         5 PA 3     .12 Z 2 1945
 9            5         4 PQ 8     .14 E 22 1986
10            6         6 PQ 77    .49 D 3 1987
11            7         7 PZ 1     .123 P 1974
12            8         8 PZ 1     .123 P 1975
13            9         9 PZ 1     .14 P 1976
14           10        10 PZ 1     .2 P1973
15
16
17
18
19
20
30-Nov-88  10:34 AM
```

'/frshelves~

This macro displays the messages enclosed in quotation marks, one at a time. The cells indicated are empty, as required for the {GETLABEL} command. Finally, after the user has read the messages, s/he is given another chance: Lotus is instructed to retrieve the file (/fr: file retrieve) named shelves (which is the name of the file that was being worked on). A return (~) completes the command, and the current file is replaced on screen with the file named shelves.

If the above-explained error was not made, the /xi statement tells Lotus to continue by going to the macro named \h.

Macro \h uses another /xi statement:

'/xib9=4~/xg\d~
'/xg\b~

In other words, if cell B9 contains the number 4, continue operating by invoking macro \d, which gives the following messages:

{GETLABEL "Before decimal point, if letters are same, smaller number first. Enter",aa13}~
{GETLABEL "Try again. Enter",aa14}~
'/frshelves~

If the user was confused about the order of call numbers before the decimal point, the messages enclosed in quotation marks would be displayed. Then, the user is given another chance; the file named shelves is retrieved (/fr: file retrieve) once again.

If this error was not made, the macro continues operation by invoking macro \b. This macro tests whether the user has gotten the last call number correct by using another /xi statement:

'/xib14<>10~/xg\a~
'/xg\e~

Once again, macro \a is invoked if cell B14 does not contain 10. Macro \a displays the messages listed above, and ends with the user being given a chance to try again, at which point the file shelves is retrieved (/fr: file retrieve).

If the final call number is correct, macro \e is invoked using the /xg\e command. Macro \e tests to see if cell B5 is greater than 2. This time, the test is to see that the user knows that a single letter preceeds multiple letters (in other words, P preceeds PA) If it is, macro \f is invoked; if not, macro \g is invoked:

'/xib5>2~/xg\f~
'/xg\g~

Macro \f displays several messages using the {GETLABEL} command.

{GETLABEL "A single letter always preceeds that letter with another. Enter",aa8}~
{GETLABEL "Therefore, P 234 will be before PA 3. Enter",aa9}~
{GETLABEL "Try again. Enter",aa10}~
'/frshelves~

Once again, after all the messages are displayed, the file shelves is retrieved (/fr: file retrieve).

If this particular error has not been made, Lotus continues operation with macro \g. This macro has only a one line message, posted using the {GETLABEL} command:

{GETLABEL "Good work: you are ready to shelve books",m1}~
{QUIT}~

In other words, once Lotus has checked for all the errors and has found the call numbers in perfect order, the user is told that s/he is ready to shelve books. The macro is then instructed to quit operation.

Each of the macros must be named, using the /rnc (range name create) command. When naming a macro, place the cursor on the first line of the macro before using /rnc (range name create). In this way, when the range is requested, you need only depress the enter key since only the first line of a macro needs to be indicated as its range.

Once all the macros have been entered and tested, it is a good idea to protect them by using /rp (range protect), /ri (range input) or /wch (worksheet column hide). The last option is only available on the more recent releases of Lotus.

Several modifications can be made: several files can be designed, each one teaching and reinforcing a particularly confusing point in shelving. In this case, at the completion of one file, Lotus would automatically retrieve the next file in the sequence. (Thus, if the

Figure 25-3

FIGURE 25-3

```
F5:   '\c
G5:   '/dsrdb5..d14~pc5..c14~a~sd5..d14~a~g
G6:   '/mb9..d9~b4~
G7:   '/mb10..d10~b9~
G8:   '/mb4..d4~b10~
G9:   '/dfa5..a14~1~1~10~
G10:  '{GETLABEL Check columns A (correct) and B (yours). Then enter ,m1}~
G11:  '/xib5=2#and#b6=1~/xg\a~
G12:  '/xg\h~
F14:  '\h
G14:  '/xib9=4~/xg\d~
G15:  '/xg\b~
F18:  '\b
G18:  '/xib14<>10~/xg\a~
G19:  '/xg\e~
F21:  '\e
G21:  '/xib5>2~/xg\f~
G22:  '/xg\g~
F24:  '\g
G24:  '{GETLABEL "Good work: You are ready to shelve books",aa15}~
G25:  '{QUIT}~
```

first file was called one, at the successful completion of that file, Lotus would be given the command /frtwo~, file retrieve two, if the next file in the sequence was named two.)

In addition, you can very easily use Dewey numbers instead of Library of Congress call numbers; the principles are exactly the same.

26 INDEXES

PROBLEM
Can Lotus be used to reinforce a lesson on the use of library indexes?

COMMANDS
Copy (/c: chapter 3)
Move (/m: chapter 4)
Range erase (/re: chapter 2)
Range input (/ri: chapter 2)
Range name create (/rnc: chapter 2)
Range protect (/rp: chapter 2)
Worksheet column hide (/wch: chapter 1)
Worksheet column-width set (/wcs: chapter 1)

CONCEPTS
Macros (chapter 13)

Though Lotus was not designed as a tool for bibliographic instruction, it is possible to use Lotus to reinforce a lesson on the use of indexes. *Readers' Guide to Periodical Literature* was chosen for the example.

The worksheet should be divided into three parts:

1. The first part contains sample citations;
2. The second, the macros used to reinforce the lesson;
3. The third, lines which are inserted into the citations of the first part.

The index citations given in the sample are in columns A and B. The column widths have been adjusted (/wcs: worksheet column-width set) as follows: column A: 2; column B: 50. These adjustments enable the screen display to approximate the citations' look in the index. Cell A1 begins the subject citation; cell A24 begins the author citation. These have been spaced so that the user will not be able to view both of the citations simultaneously unless the macros permit.

The macro portion utilizes several commands:

'/xl: This command permits the posting of messages, which are seen by the viewer in the control panel (the area in which the menu choices are usually displayed). The general format for this command is: '/xlMessage˜cell location˜, where the cell location is any unused cell. Those using the later releases of Lotus can use {GETLABEL} instead of /xl. The format for the {GETLABEL} command is: {GETLABEL "Message",cell location}˜.

'/xm: This command enables the person designing the application to create custom menus, permitting the user to choose the direction of the program's flow. The general format for the command is: '/xmCell location˜. The cell location is the top left-hand cell of the custom designed menu. Those using the later releases of Lotus can use {MENUBRANCH}. The format for the {MENUBRANCH} command is: {MENUBRANCH cell location}.

'/xg: This command instructs Lotus to continue operation at a specified location. The general format for this command is: '/xgcell location˜, where the location can be either a cell address (such as F21) or a named range (such as the macro \c).

'/re: This command erases the contents of specified cells. The general format for this command is: '/rerange˜, where the range refers to a particular cell or range of cells.

'/m: This command moves the contents of specified cells from one location to another. The general format of this command is '/mrange˜range˜, where the first range specifies the cells to be

148 USING LOTUS 1-2-3

moved, and the second specifies the range to which the cells are to be moved.

'/c: This command copies the contents of a cell from one location to another. The general format for this command is the same as the '/m command: '/crange˜range˜.

{GOTO} and {HOME}: These commands move the cursor, thus controlling what the user sees on the screen. The general format for the {GOTO} command is: {GOTO}cell location˜; the {HOME} command is simply followed by a ˜.

The beginning macro is named \0 so that it will be executed whenever this file is retrieved. To name a macro, you must use the /rnc (range name create) command. If you have your cursor on the first line of the macro, naming the range is simplified because you merely need to depress the enter key: only the first cell of a macro needs to be specified.

The first command is {HOME}˜. This command moves the cursor so that the display is on the first of the citations, in this example the subject citation. The first displayed message, using the /xl command, tells the viewer that there are two basic types of entries in this index: subject and author. When the user depresses the enter key, the sample author entry is copied from its location and both entries can now be seen. The command used to accomplish this is:

'/ca24..b26˜a10˜

After a few more comments (using /xl commands), the user is confronted with a choice of which entry to review first: subject or author. This is accomplished by using a /xm command:

'/xmf8˜

Beginning in cell F8 is the following menu:

Subject / Author
Articles about / Articles by

The user can choose by either moving the highlighting by using the arrow keys and then depressing the enter key, or by depressing the first letter of the choice. The second line is used to explain each choice.

When the choice is made, the copied citation is erased (using '/re), and, if author was chosen, the cursor is moved to cell A24 (using {GOTO}a24˜).

Figure 26-1

```
FIGURE 26-1

E14:                                                                    READY

              E              F              G              H
1    \a              {HOME}
2                    /xlIndex has 2 types of entries.Enter~k1~
3                    /ca24..b26~a10~
4                    /xlTop one is a subject entry.Enter~k2~
5                    /xlBottom is author entry.Enter~k3~
6                    /xlWhich do you want to study first?Enter~k2~
7                    /xmf8~
8                    Subject        Author
9                    Articles about Articles by
10                   /rea10..b12~   /rea10..b12~
11                   /xg\b~         {GOTO}A24~
12                                  /xg\c~
13
14
15
16
17
18
19
20
30-Nov-88  10:35 AM
```

The /xg command is used to complete each of the menu choices: '/xg\b~ and '/xg\c~, where \b and \c are named macros. One continues with the examination of the subject citation, while the other continues with the examination of the author citation.

Using /xl commands, messages are posted describing the different parts of each of the citations. Different parts are placed all in capital letters, using the /m command, where the information in capital letters was in the third part of the worksheet, moved to the appropriate citation, and later moved back. For example, to show the title all in capital letters in a subject citation, the following commands were written:

'/mb2~z3~
'/mz2~b2~

Cell Z3 contains the information from cell B2, modified to show the title in capital letters. After the illustration is explained, the information is moved back where it came from in order to have the worksheet ready for the next user:

FIGURE 26-2

```
E1:  '\a
F1:  '{HOME}
F2:  '/xlIndex has 2 types of entries.Enter~k1~
F3:  '/ca24..b26~a10~
F4:  '/xlTop one is a subject entry.Enter~k2~
F5:  '/xlBottom is author entry.Enter~k3~
F6:  '/xlWhich do you want to study first?Enter~k2~
F7:  '/xmf8~
F8:  'Subject
G8:  'Author
F9:  'Articles about
G9:  'Articles by
F10: '/rea10..b12~
G10: '/rea10..b12~
F11: '/xg\b~
G11: '{GOTO}A24~
G12: '/xg\c~
E14: '\b
F14: '/xlHere subject is on top line.Enter~k10~
F15: '/xlTitle of article begins next line.Enter~k11~
F16: '/mb2~z3~
F17: '/mz2~b2~
F18: '/xlTitle is now in CAPS.Enter~k14~
F19: '/xlPeriod ends title.Enter~k15~
F20: '/mb2~z2~
F21: '/mz3~b2~
F22: '/ca24..b26~a10~
F23: '/xlTitle:new line in all entries.Enter~k22~
F24: '/rea10..b12~
F25: '/xg\d~
E27: '\d
F27: '/xlAfter first period: author.Enter~k21~
F28: '/xlSometimes name is not given.Enter~k22~
F29: '/mb2~z6~
F30: '/mz5~b2~
F31: '/xlNow author's name is in CAPS.Enter~k25~
F32: '/xlPeriod ends author's name.Enter~k26~
F33: '/mb2~z5~
F34: '/mz6~b2~
F35: '/xg\e~
E38: '\e
F38: '/xlAfter author's name: il.Enter~k38~
F39: '/xlil means illustrated.Enter~k39~
F40: '/xlIf il not there: no illustration.Enter~k40~
F41: '/xlThen: abbreviated journal name.Enter~k41~
F42: '/mb2..b3~z22~
F43: '/mz20..z21~b2~
F44: '/xlNow journal is in CAPS.Enter~K44~
F45: '/xlAbbrev explained: index beginning.Enter~k45~
F46: '/mb2..b3~z20~
```

Continued

FIGURE 26-2 Continued

```
F47:  '/mz22..z23~b2~
F48:  '/xg\f~
E51:  '\f
F51:  '/xlNow: when published and pages.Enter~k51~
F52:  '/cz30..z34~b7~
F53:  '/xlExamine notes.Enter~k53~
F54:  '/reb7..b11~
F55:  '/xg\g~
E57:  '\g
F57:  '/xlDo you want to continue?Enter~k57~
F58:  '/xmf59~
F59:  'Subject
G59:  'Author
F60:  'Articles about
G60:  'Articles by
F61:  '/rea10..b12~
G61:  '/rea10..b12~
F62:  '{HOME}~
G62:  '{GOTO}A24~
F63:  '/xg\b~
G63:  '/xg\c~
E65:  '\c
F65:  '/xlAuthor's name on top line.Enter~k65~
F66:  '/xlTitle of article begins next line.Enter~k11~
F67:  '/mb25~z40~
F68:  '/mz41~b25~
F69:  '/xlTitle is now in CAPS.Enter~k14~
F70:  '/xlPeriod ends title.Enter~k15~
F71:  '/mb25~z41~
F72:  '/mz40~b25~
F73:  '/ca1..b3~a30~
F74:  '/xlTitle:new line in all entries.Enter~k22~
F75:  '/rea30..b32~
F76:  '/xg\h~
E79:  '\h
F79:  '/xlNext: il.Enter~k79~
F80:  '/xlil means illustrated.Enter~k39~
F81:  '/xlIf il not there: no illustration.Enter~k40~
F82:  '/xlThen: abbreviated journal name.Enter~k41~
F83:  '/mb25~z51~
F84:  '/mz50~b25~
F85:  '/xlNow journal is in CAPS.Enter~K44~
F86:  '/xlAbbrev explained: index beginning.Enter~k45~
F87:  '/mb25~z50~
F88:  '/mz51~b25~
F89:  '/xg\i~
E91:  '\i
F91:  '/xlNow: when published and pages.Enter~k51~
F92:  '/cz30..z34~b30~
F93:  '/xlExamine notes.Enter~k53~
F94:  '/reb30..b34~~
F95:  '/xg\g~
```

'/mb2~z2~
'/mz3~b2~

The citation is now restored to its original condition.

Messages are posted (using /xl commands) to explain each of the citations' parts, and when the user confronts the numbers that detail the volume, page, and date of publication, explanatory notes are copied from the third part of the worksheet:

'/cz30..z34~b20~

Cells Z30 through Z34 contain the information. Since it was copied rather than moved, it can be erased after it is viewed (using '/re: range erase); it will still be available for the next user.

The macros should be protected: /rp (range protect) or /ri (range input), or /wch (worksheet column hide) for those using the later releases of Lotus.

Figure 26-2

27 CATALOG CARDS

PROBLEM
Can Lotus be used to reinforce a lesson on what information can be found on a library catalog card?

COMMANDS
Copy (/c: chapter 3)
Move (/m: chapter 4)
Range name create (/rnc: chapter 2)
Worksheet column-width set (/wcs: chapter 1)

CONCEPTS
Macros (chapter 13)

Though Lotus was not designed as a teaching tool, you can construct a worksheet to be used to reinforce a lesson on the card catalog. The worksheet should be divided into three parts:

1. The first will contain samples of catalog cards.
2. The second will contain the many macros necessary.
3. The third part will be used to maneuver information.

Each of these parts will be discused individually.

The first part, which in the sample occupies columns A and B, contains reproductions of catalog cards, one author, one subject, and one title, all for the same book. They are spaced so that they cannot be seen simultaneously. The author card has been placed beginning in cell A3. The subject card begins in cell A24. The title card begins in cell A50. Column B was widened (/wcs: worksheet column-width set) to 60 to accommodate the body of the card. It cannot be made wider: the entire card should be visible at one time.

The second part of the worksheet is devoted to the many macros written to help reinforce the lesson on the contents of a catalog card. The macro commands in all of these statements are:

'/xl: In this set of macros, this command is used to post messages to the user; the messages appear in the panel above the sample cards. The general form of this command is '/xlMessage˜cell location˜. The cell location is any blank cell; in these macros the cell will remain empty, since the response to these /xl messages is simply to depress the enter key. If you are using a recent release of Lotus, you can use the {GETLABEL} command, which can post longer messages than the /xl command. The /xl command begins with a label prefix ('): a label prefix is necessary in this command so that Lotus does not immediately retrieve a menu, which the / would normally invoke.

'/xm: This command is used to create user-defined menus. The general form of this command is: '/xmCell location˜. The cell location is the left-most choice of the first line of the user-designed menu. In the more recent releases of Lotus, you can use the {MENUBRANCH} command. In a macro, the /xm command begins with a label prefix (').

'/xg: This command tells Lotus to continue operation at a designated location. The general format of this command is '/xgCell location˜. The cell location can be either a particular cell address or a named range such as a macro. If the /xg command is used with a named macro, the form is '/xg\a˜. In a macro, the /xg command begins with a label prefix (').

{GOTO} and {HOME}: These commands move the cursor. The

general format for these commands is {GOTO}Cell location˜ and {HOME}˜. The cell location can be either a particular cell or a named range.

The first macro is named twice: \0, which means that it is automatically executed every time this worksheet is retrieved, and \a, so that it can be invoked during the session. The first command is {HOME}˜, which moves the cursor to the home position. On the screen the user can see the first of the sample library catalog cards; in the sample, this is an author card.

Figure 27-1

While the card is on the screen, the /xl command displays messages. These messages are seen in the control panel, located at the top of the screen, where the menus are usually displayed. The first message asks what type of card is being displayed and then an /xm command is given, which provides a user-designed menu, whose choices are author, title, and subject. Under each choice, and displayed when each of the choices is highlighted, are explanations of the highlighted menu choice.

Figure 27-2

Depending on which menu choice is made, the macro continues by going to another macro, using the /xg command. If author is

---

FIGURE 27-1

```
A1:                                                              READY

             A                              B
 1
 2
 3     QA
 4     29         Baum, Joan, 1937-
 5     .L72         The calculating passion of Ada Byron / Joan Baum. -- Hamden
 6     B38       Conn., Shoe String, c1986.
 7     1986        xix, 133p. ; 23 cm.
 8                 Includes bibliography and index
 9                 ISBN 0-208-02119-1
10
11
12
13
14              1. Lovelace, Ada King, Countess of, 1815-1852.
15              2. Mathematicians--Great Britain--Biography. 3. Calculators--
16              History. 4. Computers--History. I. Title.
17
18
19
20
30-Nov-88  10:35 AM
```

> **FIGURE 27-2**
>
> ```
> {HOME}~
> /xlWhat type of card is this? Enter~H1~
> /xmd4~
> Author                    Title                     Subject
> Author's name on first line   Title on first line       Subject on first line
> /xg\b~                    /xg\c~                    /xg\d~
> ```
>
> Worksheet printed using Sideways

chosen, the next line is '/xg\b˜. If title is chosen, the next line is '/xg\c˜. If subject is chosen, the next line is '/xg\d˜.

The macro invoked by chosing title continues by explaining that this card is not a title card, but rather an author card, using /xl commands. The user is then shown a title card, using the {GOTO} command, which moves the cursor to the location of the title card. The user can then see the difference between the author card, which was displayed at the beginning, and the title card which is now displayed. Here a message is posted explaining that the title is on the top line of the title card. Then the user is returned to the author card, using a {GOTO} command. The macro continues execution with an /xg command, which directs the macro to continue operation in cell D9, which is where the user who correctly answered the initial question about the type of card being displayed was sent after a congratulatory message.

The macro invoked by choosing subject is handled in a similar manner as title, but instead of a title card being displayed, a subject card is. The cursor is moved using the {GOTO} command, and messages are posted using /xl commands. Before the macro continues operation, the cursor is returned to the author card, using the {HOME} command.

The macro continues operation with a message (using the /xl command) asking for the author's first name, and a choice is given using the /xm command. In the sample, if Joan is picked, the macro continues operation with the macro named \f; if Baum was picked, macro \e is invoked.

Finally the title's first two words are asked for (using the /xl command), and a menu choice is given (using a /xm command). If the wrong choice is made, the macro instructs the user to try again (using an /xl command) and loops back to the beginning of this macro (using the '/xg\g˜ command; this macro was named \g). The last word of the title is treated in the same manner, with messages (/xl), a menu (/xm), and a loop (provided by a /xg command).

Using the move command (/m), the macro then moves the original line with the title to the third section of the worksheet and moves a modified line with the title all in capital letters to the sample author card. The sequence used is:

'/mb5~z7~
'/mz6~b5~

Cell Z6 had the title all in capital letters. This line was prepared originally by using the copy command (/c) to copy cell B5, and then modifications were made.

At this point, the macro displays a message informing the user that the title is now all in CAPS, followed by an explanation that this is just to illustrate where the title is on this card. Then the card has to be restored, using the move command (/m) several times:

'/mb5~z7~
'/mz5~b5~
'/mz7~z6~

The final move is to prepare the worksheet for the next potential user.

The copyright year is asked for, and a menu is given. Once again, if the wrong choice is made, the user can try again. The /xg command is used to provide a loop.

The publisher's name and place of publication are then placed all in CAPS, for illustrative purposes only. This is accomplished by using the move command (/m) several times:

'/mb5..b6~z10~
'/mz12..z13~b5~

The cells Z12 and Z13 contain the lines from cells B5 and B6 with the publisher's name and place of publication in capital letters. To prepare these cells, the copy command (/c) was used, and the necessary modifications were made.

The sample author card then has to be restored, using the move command (/m) several times:

'/mb5..b6~z14~
'/mz10..z11~b5~
'/mz14..z15~z12~

FIGURE 27-3

```
C1:  '\a
D1:  '{HOME}~
I1:  '\c
J1:  '/xlBaum, Joan is not the title. Enter~11~
D2:  '/xlWhat type of card is this? Enter~H1~
J2:  '/xlBaum, Joan is the author. Enter~12~
D3:  '/xmd4~
J3:  '/xlThus, this is an author card~13~
D4:  'Author
E4:  'Title
F4:  'Subject
J4:  '/xlEnter to see a title card~14~
D5:  'Author's name on first line
E5:  'Title on first line
F5:  'Subject on first line
J5:  '{GOTO}a50~
D6:  '/xg\b~
E6:  '/xg\c~
F6:  '/xg\d~
J6:  '/xlTitle is on top line. Enter~16~
J7:  '{HOME}~
C8:  '\b
D8:  '/xlCorrect: This is an author card. Enter~H7~
J8:  '/xgd9~
D9:  '/xlWhat is the author's first name? Enter~h8~
D10: '/xmd11~
I10: '\f
J10: '/xlYes: top line last name is first. Enter~17~
D11: 'Baum
E11: 'Joan
J11: '/xgd16~
D12: 'First name?
E12: 'First name?
D13: '/xg\e~
E13: '/xg\f~
I13: '\d
J13: '/xlBaum, Joan is not the subject. Enter~11~
C14: '\e
J14: '/xlBaum, Joan is the author. Enter~12~
D15: '/xlSorry: Baum is the last name.Enter~h14~
J15: '/xlThus, this is an author card~13~
D16: '/xlJoan is the first name.Enter~h16~
J16: '/xlEnter to see a subject card~113~
D17: '/xg\g~
J17: '{GOTO}a25~
J18: '/xlSubject is on top line. Enter~115~
C19: '\g
D19: '/xlTitle's first 2 words are? Enter~h19~
J19: '{HOME}~
D20: '/xmd21~
J20: '/xgd9~
D21: 'The calculating
E21: 'Ada Byron
F21: 'Shoe String
D22: 'First two?
E22: 'First two?
```

Continued

158 USING LOTUS 1-2-3

FIGURE 27-3 *Continued*

```
F22: 'First two?
D23: '/xg\h~
E23: '/xlTry again. Enter~h23~
F23: '/xlTry again. Enter~h23~
E24: '/xg\g~
F24: '/xg\g~
C27: '\h
D27: '/xlLast word of title? Enter~h27~
D28: '/xmd29~
D29: 'String
E29: 'Ct
F29: 'Ada
G29: 'Byron
D30: 'Last word of title?
E30: 'Last word of title?
F30: 'Last word of title?
G30: 'Last word of title?
D31: '/xlTry again. Enter~h31~
E31: '/xlTry again. Enter~h31~
F31: '/xlTry again. Enter~h31~
G31: '/xg\i~
D32: '/xg\h~
E32: '/xg\h~
F32: '/xg\h~
C35: '\i
D35: '/mb5~z5~
D36: '/mz6~b5~
D37: '/xlThe entire title is now in CAPS. Enter~h35~
D38: '/xlThis is just for now~h36~
D39: '/xlNormally titles are not all CAPS. Enter~h37~
D40: '/mb5~z7~
D41: '/mz5~b5~
D42: '/mz7~z6~
D43: '/xg\j~
C45: '\j
D45: '/xlYear of copyright? Enter~b31~
D46: '/xmd47~
D47: 'a.1815
E47: 'b.1986
F47: 'c.1852
G47: 'd.1937
D48: 'Copyright year?
E48: 'Copyright year?
F48: 'Copyright year?
G48: 'Copyright year?
D49: '/xlTry again. Enter~H39~
E49: '/xg\k~
F49: '/xlTry again. Enter~H39~
G49: '/xlThis is author's birth year. Enter~h49~
D50: '/xg\j~
F50: '/xg\j~
G50: '/xlTry again~h49~
G51: '/xg\j~
C53: '\k
D53: '/xlYes: c1986 means copyright 1986. Enter~h53~
D54: '/xlBefore c1986 is publisher's name. Enter~h54~
```

Continued

FIGURE 27-3 *Continued*

```
D55:  '/xlBefore that: publication place.Enter~h55~
D56:  '/mb5..b6~z10~
D57:  '/mz12..z13~b5~
D58:  '/xlPub's name & place now in CAPS. Enter~h35~
D59:  '/xlThis is just for now~h36~
D60:  '/xlNormally they are not all CAPS. Enter~h37~
D61:  '/mb5..b6~z14~
D62:  '/mz10..z11~b5~
D63:  '/mz14..z15~z12~
D64:  '/xg\l~
C66:  '\l
D66:  '/xlNext: number of pages & height. Enter~h66~
I66:  '\m
J66:  '/xlTo find book.Enter~m66~
D67:  '/xlBibliography and index noted. Enter~h67~
J67:  '/xmj68~
D68:  '/xlLook at very bottom of card. Enter~h68~
J68:  'B section
K68:  'C section
L68:  'QA section
D69:  '/xlNumbers are subjects of book. Enter~h69~
J69:  'Look here
K69:  'Look here
L69:  'Look here
D70:  '/xlThere are 4 subject headings.Enter~h70~
J70:  '/xlLocation is in upper left corner.Enter~m70~
K70:  '/xlLocation is in upper left corner.Enter~m70~
L70:  '/xlCorrect: the QA section. Enter~m70~
D71:  '/mb14..b16~z25~
J71:  '/xlBook is in QA section.Enter~m71~
K71:  '/xlBook is in QA section.Enter~m71~
L71:  '/xlLocation is in upper left corner.Enter~m70~
D72:  '/mz20..z22~b14~
J72:  '/xg\n~
K72:  '/xg\n~
L72:  '/xg\n~
D73:  '/xlSubjects are now in CAPS. Enter~h73~
D74:  '/xlThis is just for now. Enter~h74~
D75:  '/xlNormally they are not all CAPS. Enter~h75~
D76:  '/mb14..b16~z30~
D77:  '/mz25..z27~b14~
D78:  '/mz30..z32~z20~
D79:  '/xg\m~
C81:  '\n
D81:  '/xlTitle & subject cards are same.Enter~h81~
D82:  '/xlExcept top line. Enter~h82~
D83:  '{GOTO}a50~
D84:  '/xlThis is a title card. Enter~h84~
D85:  '/xlTitle on top line. Enter~h85~
D86:  '{GOTO}a25~
D87:  '/xlThis is a subject card.Enter~h87~
D88:  '/xlOne subject on top line.Enter~h88~
D89:  '/xlEach of the 4 subjects has a card.Enter~h89~
D90:  '/xmd91~
D91:  'Author
E91:  'Title
```

Continued

```
FIGURE 27-3 Continued

F91:  'Subject
G91:  'Entire lesson
D92:  'View card
E92:  'View card
F92:  'View card
G92:  'Restart
D93:  '{HOME}~
E93:  '{GOTO}a50~
F93:  '{GOTO}a25~
G93:  '/xg\a~
D94:  '/xgd90~
E94:  '/xgd90~
F94:  '/xgd90~
```

The final move readies the worksheet for the next potential user.

Other features of the author card are noted, using the /xl command. The four subject headings (tracings) on the bottom of the card are mentioned and highlighted by putting them all in capital letters; the move command (/m) is used.

The location of the book in the library is then questioned, using a user defined menu (/xm), which asks in which section of the library the book can be found. Incorrect choices are looped to permit the user to try again. The correct choice continues the lesson.

Then the user is shown both a subject card and a title card. The cursor is moved using {GOTO} commands. When each is viewed, a message explaining the differences between the types of cards is displayed (using the /xl command).

Finally, the user is given the chance to view each of the three types of cards, or to review the entire lesson. This choice is provided using a /xm command. After each type of card is seen, the macro loops back to this menu, where the user can again view each of the types of cards. If the final choice is made, to review the entire lesson, the \a macro is invoked ('/xg\a˜); this macro begins the lesson again.

Each of the macros must be named individually by using the range name create command (/rnc). Each of the macros is named with a \ and a letter of the alphabet: only single letters can be used. When naming a macro, it is helpful to place the cursor on the first cell in that macro because when asked for the range, the enter key can simply be depressed. Only the first cell in a macro needs to be specified.

Figure 27-3

Robert Machalow is Assistant Professor at York College Library, City University of New York, Jamaica, and Contributing Editor, *Small Computers in Libraries* (Meckler).

Bill Katz is a Professor at the School of Library and Information Science and Policy, State University of New York at Albany, and author of over 15 books, including the two-volume *Reference and Online Services Handbook* (Neal-Schuman).

Book design: Gloria Brown
Typography: Roberts/Churcher

INDEX

Absolute cell addresses, 25, 67, 79–80, 98, 113
Adding new entries in lists, 103–104
Addition, 46, 75, 78, 98, 113, 118
Addresses, worksheet for, 85
ALIGN (/ppa), 38
ALIGN (graphs), 42
Amounts paid, worksheet for, 67–68
Anchoring range ends, 25
AND operator, 47
Apostrophe, use of, 15
Arrow keys, use of, 14
At sign (formulas), 46
Auto-execute macro name, 57
Average numbers function, 47
AVG function, 47

B&W (graphs), 40
Bar graph macros, 61
Bar graphs (/gtb), 40
Bar graphs, 52
BEEP, use of in macros, 59, 61
Bibliographic instruction
  catalog cards, worksheet for, 153–160
  periodical indexing services, worksheet for, 147–152
  software for, worksheet for, 130–139
Bills (approximate), worksheet for, 67
Bin ranges, 72
Blank spaces, filling of, 14
Book budgets
  pie chart for, 76
  worksheet for, 74–76
Borders, 37
Budget remainders (approximate), worksheet for, 67
Budget requests, worksheet for, 79–82
Budgets, worksheet for, 77–78

Catalog cards, instruction in use of, worksheet for, 153–160
Cell, definition of, 14

Cell addresses
  effect of moving on, 28
  types of, 25
Cell contents, changing of, 54
Change permission, 56
Change restriction, 56
Charges for database searching, worksheet for, 118–129
Circulation, worksheet for, 85–97
Circulation list updating, macro for, 95–96
CLEAR (/ppc), 38
Color (graphs), 40
Column alignment, 29
Column headings
  on screen, 50
  underlining of, 71
Column headings modification, 31
COLUMN WIDTH (/wgc), 19
Column width adjustments, 29
COLUMN-WIDTH (/wc), 20
Column widths, 49
Columns
  insertion of, 20
  macro for insertion of, 58
COMBINE (/fc), 35
Comma format, 18
Commands
  review of, 54–56
  summary of (table), 55
COPY (/c), 25–26
Copy command, 46, 54
  use of, 25
Copying, shortcut method, 26
Create names, 23
Criterion range (/dqc), 44
Currency, formatting for, 70
Currency format, 18, 29, 49
Cursor, movement of, 14

DATA (/d), 43–45
Data distribution (/dd), 72
Data fill (/df), 50
Data labels (graphs), 40
Data query extract (/dqe), 50, 51
Data query find (/dqf), 50
Data sort (/ds), 50
Database searching, administrative records of, worksheets for, 118–129

DATE, use of in worksheets, 98
Date format, 18, 49
DATE function, 48, 83, 98, 118
DAVG function, 127
DCOUNT function, 127
Decimal format, 18
DEFAULT (/wgd), 19
Default disk, change of, 19
DELETE (/wd), 20
Delete names, 23
Delete option (/dqd), 44
Deletion, 54
Delivery dates, worksheet for, 67
Department budgets, worksheet for, 67–73
Dewey call numbers, worksheet for, 146
DIRECTORY (/fd), 35
Display, 20
Display format, 18
DISTRIBUTION (/dd), 45
Division, 46, 98, 113, 116, 130
  remainders in, 46–47
  rounding off numbers in, 47
  whole numbers in, 47
DMAX function, 127
DMIN function, 127
DSUM function, 127

End key, 14, 85, 103, 106
Enter key, use of in copying, 26
Equal sign, 47
ERASE (/fe), 35
ERASE (/re), 22
ERASE (/we), 20
Erasing, 54
Exit (/qy), 41
EXIT (graphs), 42
Extract option (/dqe), 44

F1 key, 17
  help for macros, 58
F2 key, 54
F5 key, 14, 26
F6 key, 20
F9 key, 19
FILE (/f), 34–35
File erase (/fe), 54

163

File save (/fs), 54, 56
Files
　access to through passwords, 34–35
　names of existing, 35
　naming of, 34
　saving of, 34–35
FILL (/df), 43
Fines
　allowance for days closed, 99
　computation of, worksheet for, 98–102
Fixed format, 18
Font sizes, 37
Font styles, 37
Footers, 37
Form letters, worksheet for, 85–97
FORMAT (/rf), 22
FORMAT (/wgf), 18
Format (graphs), 40
Formats, choices, 18
Formatted style, 37
Formatting, 54
Formulas, 46–48
　names for, 23
Functions, 46–48

General format, 18
GETLABEL, 130
GETNUMBER, 130
GLOBAL (/wg), 18
GLOBAL PROTECT (/wgp), 24
GO (/ppg), 38
GO (graphs), 41
GOTO key, 14, 25–26
GRAPH (/g), 39–42
Graph save (/gs), 56
Graphing, 52–53
Greater than sign, 47
Grid (graphs), 40

Headers, 37
Help key, 17
　macro instructions found on, 58
Hidden format, 18
Hide, 20
Hiding of macros, 101

Highlighter, movement of, 14
Highlighting requirements for, 72
Home key, 14

IF function, 47–48, 100, 119, 135
IMPORT (/fi), 35
INPUT (/ri), 24
Input range (/dqi), 44
INSERT (/wi), 20
Inserting a column, macro for, 58
Inserting a row, macro for, 58–59
Insertion, 54
INT function, 47, 83, 100
Interactive macros, 57–58
Interactive sort, macro for, 59
Invoice dates, worksheet for, 67

JUSTIFY (/rj), 23

Label names, 23
LABEL PREFIX (/rl), 22
LABEL PREFIX (/wgl), 19
Label prefixes, 57
Left hand justification, 15
Legends, 40
Lesser than sign, 47
Letters, worksheet for, 85–97
Library applications, 65–160
Library budgets, worksheet for, 77–78
Library materials, worksheet for, 77–78
Library of Congress call numbers, worksheet for, 146
LINE (/ppl), 37
Line graphs (/gtl), 40
LIST (/fl), 35
Lists, updating of, 103–104
Lists of periodicals held, worksheet for, 103–112
Logical operators, 47
Loops
　breaking out of, 92
　use of in macros, 89

Macros
　for bar graphs, 61
　basics of, 57–61
　for catalog card instruction, 153–160
　for database search records, 118–129
　differences between LOTUS releases for, 130, 133, 134, 135
　editing of, 57
　examples of, 58–61
　for exiting Lotus after file replacement, 60
　for form letters, 85–97
　hiding of, 101
　for insertion of rows or columns, 58–59
　for instruction in periodical indexing services, 147–152
　interactive, 57–58
　for interactive sorting, 59
　keywords and help for, 58
　for lists of periodicals held, 103–112
　loops in, 89
　names for, 23, 57
　naming ranges in, 58
　for overdue fines computation, 98–102
　for pie charts, 60–61
　for printing, 60
　protection of, 90–91
　for software evaluation, 130–139
　STEP MODE for, 57
　for training of shelvers, 140–146
　use of, 57
　use of BEEP, 59
　what if situations, 77–78
　writing of, 58
Margins, 37
MATRIX (/dm), 45
MAX function, 47
Maximum or minimum costs, searching for, 112
Maximum values, 47
Menu, selection from, 17
MENUBRANCH, 93, 99, 136
MIN function, 47

INDEX

Minimum or maximum costs, searching for, 112
Minimum values, 47
Mixed cell addresses, 25, 74–75, 113, 118
MOD function, 47, 83, 84
MOVE (/m), 27–28
Move (/m), 54
Moving, need for space, 27
Multiple year budget request, worksheet for, 79
Multiplication, 46, 77, 98, 130

NA function, 86
NAME (/gn), 40
NAME (/rn), 23
Name list updating, macro for, 95–96
Names
   order of in addresses, macro for, 89
   sorting of, 85
Naming of files, 34
Non-English entries, searching of, 108
Not equal sign, 47
NOT operator, 47
Number 7 key, 14

Online searches, administrative records of, worksheets for, 118–129
OPTIONS (/go), 40
OPTIONS (/ppo), 37
OR operator, 47
Order dates, worksheet for, 67
Output range (/dqo), 44–45
Overdue fines computation, worksheet for, 98–102
Overdue form letters, worksheet for, 85–97

PAGE (/ppp), 37
PAGE (/wp), 21
PAGE (graphs), 42
Page breaks, 37

Page length, 37
PARSE (/dp), 45
Part-time workers, time sheets for, 83–84
Passwords, access to files with, 34–35
Percent format, 18
Percentages, 52
   computation of, 51, 114, 116
Periodical holdings, worksheet for, 103–112
Periodical indexing services, instruction in, worksheet for, 147–152
Pie chart macros, 60–61
Pie charts (/gtp), 40
Pie charts
   for book budgets, 76
   worksheet for, 79, 82
Pie graphs, 52
Plus or minus format, 18
Point mode, 25
PRINT (/p), 36–38
Print files, incorporation of into worksheets, 35
Print macros, 60
Print to a file (/pf), 36
Print to a printer (/pp), 36
PrintGraph disk, 41
PROTECT (/rp), 23
PROTECTION (/wgp), 19
Protection of macros, 90–91

QUERY (/dq), 44
Quit, 41

RANGE (/ppr), 36–37
RANGE (/r), 22–24
Range ends, anchoring of, 25
RANGE ERASE (/re), 35, 54
Range format (/rf), 54
Range format date (/rfd), 48
Range format display (/rfd), 56
Range format hidden (/rfh), 56
Range input (/ri), 56
   for macros, 58
Range name create (/rnc), 57
Range protect (/rp), 56
   for macros, 58

Range unprotect (/ru), 56
Reader's Guide to Periodical Literature, instruction in using, worksheet for, 147–152
RECALCULATION (/wgr), 19
Reference statistics, worksheet for, 113–117
REGRESSION (/dr), 45
Relative cell addresses, 25, 67, 74–75, 79–82, 113, 118, 130
Remainders in division, 46–47
Repeat signal (\ ), 79
Replace file and exit Lotus macro, 60
RESET (/gr), 40
Reset names, 23
RETRIEVE (/fr), 35
Review of features, 49–53
Review of first four menu choices, 29–33
ROUND function, 47
Rounding off numbers in division, 47
Rows
   insertion of, 20
   macro for insertion of, 58–59
Running totals, 46, 50

Salutations in letters, macro for, 90
SAVE (/fs), 34–35
SAVE (/gs), 40
Saving, 56
Saving graphs (/gs), 40, 41
Saving of worksheets, 34–35, 50
Scale (graphs), 40
Scientific format, 18
SELECT (graphs), 41
SETTINGS (graphs), 41
Setup, 37
Shelving of books, training in, worksheet for, 140–146
Slash (/) key, 17
Software evaluation, worksheet for, 130–139
Sort (/ds), 44
Sorting of names, 85
Stacked bar graphs (/gts), 40
Statements, names for, 23

Statistics on reference work, worksheet for, 113–117
STATUS (/ws), 20
STEP MODE, for macros, 57
Submenu, location of, 17
Subtraction, 46, 75, 78, 98
SUM function, 46, 51, 74, 79, 83, 119, 136

TABLE (/dt), 44
Text format, 18
Time sheets, worksheet for, 83–84
Time worked, worksheet for, 83–84
Title (graphs), 40
TITLES (/wt), 20
TODAY function, 98, 118
Total budget spent (approximate), worksheet for, 68–69
Total budget spent, worksheet for, 69–70
TRANSPOSE (/rt), 24
Two-disk system, change of default disk in, 19
TYPE (/gt), 39

Underline column headings, 49
Underlining, 26
  of column headings, 71
Unformatted style, 37
Unique option, (/dqu), 44
UNPROTECT (/ru), 23
Updating of form letter data, macro for, 91

VALUE (/rv), 24
Vendor location, 72
Vendor records, worksheet for, 67
VIEW (/gv), 40
Visibility of column headings on screen, 29
Visibility of row titles on screen, 32–33

What if situations, macros for, 77–78
Whole numbers in division, 47
WINDOW (/ww), 20
WORKSHEET, (/W), 17–21
Worksheet
  blank, 13
  submenus available with, 18
Worksheet column display (/wcd), 56
Worksheet column hide (/wch), 56, 58
Worksheet delete column (/wdc), 54
Worksheet delete row (/wdr), 54
Worksheet erase (/we), 35, 54
Worksheet global format (/wgf), 54
Worksheet global format date (/wgfd), 48
Worksheet global protect (/wgp), 56
Worksheet insert column (/wic), 50, 54
Worksheet insert row (/wir), 54
Worksheets
  for bibliographic instruction software, 130–139
  for book budgets, 74–76
  for budget requests, 79–82
  for catalog card instruction, 153–160
  for computation of fines, 98–102
  for database searching statistics, 118–129
  for department budgets, 67–73
  erasing of, 20
  for form letters, 85–97
  for instruction in periodical indexing services, 147–152
  for library budgets, 77–78
  for lists of periodicals held, 103–112
  for reference statistics, 113–117
  saving of, 34–35, 50
  size of, 15
  for software evaluation, 130–139
  for timesheets, 83–84
  for training of shelvers, 140–146
Writeovers, 54

XTRACT (/fx), 35
XY graphs (/gtx), 40

ZERO (/wgz), 19